Why HE Kept Me

THORIS LAMAR BURT &
CAROLYN VIRGINIA BURT

Scripture quotations marked (KJV) are taken from the King James Version (public domain).

Scripture quotations marked (NIV) are taken from the Holy Bible, New International Version®, NIV®. Copyright © 1973, 1978, 1984, 2011 by Biblica, Inc.™ Used by permission. All rights reserved worldwide.

Cover and interior formatting by KUHN Design Group | kuhndesigngroup.com
Copy editing by Sally Apokedak
Proofreading by Blair Parke

Why HE Kept Me:
A Story of God's Faithfulness, Mental Health, and Miraculous Survival

Published by Arise & Declare Press | an imprint of Arise Agency, LLC | Orlando, Florida
www.whyhekeptme.com | info@whyhekeptme.com

This book is a memoir. It reflects the authors' present recollections of experiences over time. Some names and identifying details have been changed to protect the privacy of the individuals involved. Conversations have been reconstructed from memory.

This book is not a substitute for professional medical or mental-health advice. The authors are not medical or mental-health professionals. If you or someone you know is in crisis, call or text 988 (Suicide & Crisis Lifeline) or text HOME to 741741 (Crisis Text Line).

ISBN (paperback): 979-8-9964979-0-4
ISBN (hardcover): 979-8-9964979-1-1
ISBN (ebook): 979-8-9964979-2-8

First Edition, 2026

Printed in the United States of America

CONTENTS

PART IV: BREAKING: WHEN THE MIND TURNS (2018-2021)

PART V: SHATTERING: THE VALLEY OF THE SHADOW (2022-2024)

PART VI: RESTORING: SIGNS, SYMBOLS, AND THE ROAD BACK

PART VII: RESTING: THE PURPOSE BEHIND THE PAIN (2025-2026)

A NOTE BEFORE YOU BEGIN

This book reflects the lived experiences and personal journey of Thoris Lamar Burt, co-authored with Carolyn Virginia Burt. It is offered for informational, inspirational, and testimonial purposes only—to bear witness, encourage hope, and share perspective. It is not a substitute for professional care.

The mental-health experiences described in these pages are personal and contextual. They are not intended as medical, psychological, psychiatric, or therapeutic advice, nor should they be interpreted as such. Nothing in this book is intended to diagnose, treat, cure, or prevent any mental-health condition. Each person's journey is unique, and outcomes vary based on personal, medical, and professional factors.

If you are experiencing emotional distress, mental-health challenges, or thoughts of self-harm, please seek help from a qualified mental-health professional, counselor, physician, or licensed therapist. If you or someone you know is in immediate danger, contact local emergency services. In the United States, support is available 24/7 through the Suicide & Crisis Lifeline at 988—call or text.

Any references to Social Security Disability Insurance (SSDI) are shared solely as personal testimony and lived experience. They are not legal, financial, or benefits advice and should not be relied upon for guidance regarding eligibility, applications, appeals, timelines, or outcomes. SSDI rules vary by individual circumstance and are subject to change; each case is reviewed independently by the Social Security Administration. For guidance, consult the SSA, a qualified disability attorney, or a licensed financial or legal professional.

This book includes faith-based reflections, Scripture, and prayer. These expressions reflect personal belief and lived faith and are not substitutes for professional medical, mental-health, legal, or financial care. Faith and professional care are not in conflict—they can walk together.

Information regarding Crisis Intervention Teams (CIT) and Community Response Teams (CRT) is offered for general awareness only. Availability, training, and response protocols vary by jurisdiction. In an emergency, always call 911 and clearly state that the situation is a mental-health crisis; request a CIT-trained officer or CRT team if available in your area.

By reading this book, you acknowledge that you are responsible for your own health, legal, and financial decisions. The authors and publisher are not liable for actions taken based on the content presented here.

CAROLYN'S FOREWORD

A MOTHER'S PRAYER

"But my God shall supply all your needs according to his riches in glory by Christ Jesus."

PHILIPPIANS 4:19 (KJV)

My reflection on faith has always been about trusting God—believing that He would take care of my three children and me.

I worked for ten years at Alabama A&M Campus Security Department (later renamed the Alabama A&M Campus Police Department), where I served as the first secretary under the leadership of the Chief of Police Clarence R. Howard. Chief often encouraged me, telling me to go take some classes. He gave me the time to attend those classes without ever asking me to make up for the hours I missed. He even allowed me to bring my son to my office once he got out of daycare. That simple act saved me from paying for an after-school program—another blessing from God.

I remember praying, asking God to bless me with a raise. At the same time, I asked Chief Howard directly if he could increase my pay. His response was, "No, Cal," which was how he pronounced my name, since his own daughter's name was Carol.

Not long after leaving the police department, God opened a new door. I was referred to Theotis Acklin by my boyfriend, an officer of Alabama A&M Police Department. I was hired as a clerk-typist with the Word Processing Center for the federal government at Redstone Arsenal. Once again, I prayed and asked God for a raise—and this time, He answered. From that day forward, I witnessed how God always provided, always kept His promises, and always gave my children and me a better life.

And so, my prayer has always been one of gratitude. What God has done for me and my family, I know He can do for others.

THORIS'S FOREWORD

A SON'S TESTIMONY

"I shall not die, but live, and declare the works of the Lord."

PSALM 118:17 (KJV)

There are books we choose to write... and then there are books that choose us.

Why HE Kept Me is the latter.

I didn't sit down one day with a cup of tea, some outline software, and a game plan for a memoir. This book was my mother's idea. I wrote this book the way survivors breathe after resurfacing—instinctively, urgently, gratefully. Each chapter came from a moment I wasn't supposed to live through, a night that almost wasn't followed by a morning after, or a season that nearly swallowed me whole.

This book was born in therapy sessions, in hospital rooms, in silent car rides where I had to remind myself that I mattered. It grew in the pages of journals stained with tears, and in the miraculous spaces where God met me—even when I didn't know how to meet Him back.

I wrote this book because silence was suffocating me. I wrote this book because generational struggles needed language. I wrote this book because somebody is living what I lived—and thinking they're alone. I wrote this book because the stigma around mental health in our community has cost too many lives already. I wrote this book because writing was part of my healing—and now, I pray reading it becomes part of yours.

This is not a story about perfection. It's a story about preservation.

Not about how strong I was—but about how faithful God was.

Welcome to my testimony. Welcome to the truth behind the smile. Welcome to the chapters God refused to let end in tragedy.

This is why He kept me. And maybe . . . just maybe . . . this is why He kept you too.

PART I

ROOTS: WHERE FAITH WAS PLANTED

Core Teaching: God prepares you through what you survive, not despite it.

CHAPTER 1

DECATUR TO DESTINY–THE 1993 MIGRATION

Written by Carolyn Virginia Burt

"For I know the plans I have for you," declares the Lord, "plans to prosper you and not to harm you, plans to give you hope and a future."

JEREMIAH 29:11 (NIV)

I was raised in Decatur, Alabama—humble beginnings, to say the least. We were poor. We picked cotton. My father passed away when he was just 50 years old, leaving my mother to raise 7 children alone. She did the best she could with what she had and what she knew. Survival was the assignment, and somehow, she always made a way.

Most Sundays, we would go to my mother's sister's house. Aunt Tempia's husband, Uncle James, was a hunter. One Sunday, they served possum for dinner. My mother asked what kind of meat it was, and when someone told her it was possum, she threw up. Just the thought of it made her sick to her stomach.

We lived country-style: outside toilets, well water, no electricity at first, wood and coal-burning stoves. No washer or dryer: we hung our clothes on a wireline and let the sun and the wind take care of them. That was our childhood—rough, simple, and real.

My sister Marilyn and I eventually moved into the city of Decatur. Lord, that's a long story. If I started explaining why we had to stay with our first cousin, it would take all night. We stayed with my first cousin, her daughter, and her husband until life shifted again.

Later, we moved to Huntsville, Alabama, with my sister Delia—the glue that held our family together. Those were humble beginnings, too, but they shaped me. Raising children in the projects wasn't easy, but we had a village. The mothers, fathers, the neighbors, the older kids—we all looked out for one another.

I loved living in Searcy Homes—the old projects and the new ones. I lived on Dallas Avenue, Monroe Street, and Holmes Avenue. All of my children were born in the projects: Tracy in 1973, Thoris in 1977, and Terrell in 1986. I was a single mother with three different baby daddies. I was never married. My neighbors became extended family. We watched each other's children like they were our own.

One of my neighbor's daughters—a beautiful, little girl I used to babysit—sent me a picture on Facebook of a bologna and cheese sandwich and asked, "Ms. Carolyn, was this the sandwich you used to make for us?"

I told her yes—I always gave them all-beef bologna.

She laughed and told me, "Ms. Carolyn . . . we were vegetarians."

Their mother didn't even find out until 2025 that I used to feed her children meat. She said that was probably why her daughter loved staying with me so much.

I loved all the neighborhood children, but there were two sisters especially who I held close to my heart. Those were hard days—but they were good days, too. Those years taught me resilience, community, and the kind of love that doesn't break under pressure.

I prayed for God to help me move my children out of the projects. Don't get me wrong; the projects were good for us, but I wanted a better life for my children. I have always prayed to God to bless me with a good job. I never wanted my children to go hungry—to be tempted to steal from stores—or to be homeless.

We had pastors who graduated from Oakwood College, now Oakwood University, raising their families in the projects alongside single parents like me. We raised many successful children—they grew up to be military personnel, nurses, and employees of the federal government.

After I graduated in 1985 with my Bachelor of Science degree in business management, I was hired by the federal government, and I decided to move to Valley Gardens Apartments in 1989. These were basically townhomes—a major upgrade from the projects.

In 1993, after receiving some incremental promotions with the federal government, I applied for several internships, and I kept getting overlooked. One of my mentors asked me if I was willing to relocate and initially, I was reluctant because Huntsville was home, and that's where my support system was. But I prayed about it, and God spoke to me and said, "I will never leave you nor forsake you."

The very next day, I updated my resume and application to reflect I was mobile and almost instantly, I was selected for an interview and received an offer for a big promotion, but it would require me to relocate to Orlando, Florida.

I was so excited and nervous at the same time. However, I reminded myself of God's voice, "I will never leave you nor forsake you," so we packed our things and prepared for the movers to come.

September 1993 is when we drove from Huntsville to Orlando embarking on a journey to destiny. When we arrived, we were greeted by my assigned sponsor, who showed us around and made sure we were set up in a hotel upon our arrival. We instantly became friends and she and I are still friends to this day.

I could never afford to take my children to Disney World before, but suddenly we were in Disney's backyard.

A member of our home church in Huntsville, First Church, referred us to a Seventh-Day Adventist Church in Winter Park, Florida, called Patmos Chapel. Our friend had gotten to know the folks at Patmos Chapel when the Inspirational Choir was featured in a concert there. So, they came highly recommended.

After visiting a few other churches in the area, my children and I felt right at home at Patmos Chapel, so we joined.

Several members worked at Disney World and gave us free passes to the park on a regular basis.

After being in the hotel for a few months, we moved into The Woodlands Apartments until 1998 when I became a first-time homebuyer.

God blessed me to build my first home all by myself with only HIS grace and mercy. What a wonderful God we serve.

All of my life, we were poor and could not afford to buy a home. When I was a child, my family rented from Caucasians. Back then, where I was from, Black people could not afford to buy a home. I always asked God to bless me with a home that no one stayed in but my children and me. I wanted a home with 3 bedrooms, 2 baths, and a 2-car garage. And I wanted a living room, dining room, and eat-in kitchen. If I got a choice, I'd take carpet in every room except the kitchen and bathrooms—I wanted tile in those areas.

I am truly a blessed individual.

Look at God.

WHAT THIS MEANS FOR YOUR LIFE

I need you to hear something before you turn this page: Your beginning is not your ceiling.

I grew up with outside toilets, well water, and no electricity. I raised three children alone in the projects. We rented from other people my entire childhood because my family couldn't afford to own anything. If you had told me in Decatur, Alabama, that one day I would build my own home with 3 bedrooms, 2 bathrooms, and a 2-car garage, I would have laughed. Not because I didn't believe in God—but because I didn't yet believe God's plans included that level of blessing for someone like me.

That's the lie humble beginnings tell you. They whisper, "This is all you'll ever be." They convince you that poverty is prophecy. That your zip code is your destiny. That where you start is where you finish.

But Jeremiah 29:11 does not say, "I know the plans I have for you, unless you come from the projects." It does not say, "plans to prosper you, except if your daddy died young and your mama had to raise seven children alone." It says, "plans to give you hope and a future." Period.

God used my humble beginnings as preparation, not punishment. Every sacrifice I watched my mother make taught me endurance. Every neighbor who watched my children taught me community. Every year I spent in the projects taught me gratitude for what was coming.

I want to ask you something directly: What story are you telling yourself about where you come from? Are you letting your origin define your outcome? Are you believing the lie that because you started without much, you'll finish without much?

Stop it.

Your beginning is your training ground. The things that felt like limitation were building in you the very strength, faith, and hunger you will need to walk into the destiny God already prepared.

I didn't move from Huntsville to Orlando because I was brave. I moved because I prayed, and God answered. I wasn't the most qualified, the most educated, or the most connected. But I was willing. And sometimes willing is all God needs to work with.

APPLY THIS

- **Write your origin story in one paragraph.** Not the polished version. The real one. Then read it back and ask, "What did God teach me here that I couldn't have learned anywhere else?"
- **Identify the lie your beginnings told you.** Maybe it's "I'll never own anything." Maybe it's "People like me don't get those kinds of jobs." Name it. Then write the truth of Jeremiah 29:11 next to it.
- **Say yes before you're ready.** I updated my resume to say I was mobile before I felt mobile. Obedience often requires movement before confidence. What is God asking you to say yes to right now that scares you?
- **Thank God for your village.** The neighbors who watched your children. The aunt who fed you. The teacher who believed in you. Reach out to one of them this week.

IF YOU'RE IN A GROUP

- Share one specific detail about where you grew up that shaped who you are today. How do you see God's hand in that detail now?
- Have you ever let your origin story limit your expectations? What did that look like?
- Carolyn said God told her, "I will never leave you nor forsake you"—and she moved the next day. When has God spoken something to you that required immediate obedience?

Prayer: Father God, thank you for every humble beginning that prepared me for the future You planned. Forgive me for the times

I believed my starting point was my stopping point. Open doors I cannot see. Give me the courage to walk through them before I feel ready. Remind me that You have never left me and You never will. In Jesus's name. Amen.

"Humble beginnings

don't limit your destiny;

they prepare your strength.

What starts in struggle can still

rise in purpose when God's

hand is guiding the journey."

CHAPTER 2

WHEN THE HILL IS TOO STEEP

Written by Carolyn Virginia Burt

"I will lift up mine eyes unto the hills, from whence cometh my help. My help cometh from the Lord..."

PSALM 121:1-2

In 1983, I bought my very first brand-new car—a Doo-Doo Brown Ford Escort.

Stick shift.

Four-speed.

No air conditioning.

No radio.

Just me, the clutch, and a whole lot of nerves.

That car did not come with comfort; it came with responsibility.

I did not even know how to drive a manual transmission when I signed those papers. My boyfriend at the time had to teach me. And let me tell you, learning to balance a clutch and gas pedal at the same time will humble you quickly.

Every morning, I left home an hour early.

Not because I was slow.

Not because I was irresponsible.

But because I was determined not to embarrass myself.

I worked as the secretary of the Police Department at Alabama A&M University. To get there, I had to climb a steep hill just outside the office. That hill became my daily test—not just of driving skill, but of faith.

If traffic was heavy, my heart would start pounding before I even reached it. Because stopping halfway up that hill terrified me. If a car pulled up too close behind me, I would roll down my window and wave my arm, begging them to back up.

"Please give me space," I would signal, knowing that if I stalled, that car was going to feel it.

I had not yet mastered that delicate balance between clutch and gas. And the fear of rolling backward—of failing in public—felt overwhelming.

Some mornings, I prayed harder climbing that hill than I ever prayed sitting in a pew.

"Lord, don't let me stall."

"Lord, don't let me roll back."

"Lord, don't let them see me struggle."

That hill was not just pavement.

It was pressure.

It was pride.

It was perseverance.

And if I am honest, my life felt just like that car.

There were seasons when I stalled.

Seasons when I felt like I was rolling backward.

Seasons when I feared people were watching me struggle.

It took me ten years to finish my business management degree.

Ten years.

Not because I was lazy.

Not because I lacked intelligence.

But because I was working full time.

Because I was raising children.

Because I was carrying responsibilities that do not show up on transcripts.

Single parenting is a hill.

Financial strain is a hill.

Exhaustion is a hill.

There were nights I studied with one eye open.

Mornings I went to work tired but determined.

Moments I wondered if I should quit.

But I kept climbing.

Slowly.

Carefully.

Sometimes trembling.

And just like learning that clutch, I eventually figured out the rhythm.

Balance the pressure.

Ease into the gas.

Trust the timing.

Ten years later, I reached the top of that academic hill.

It did not look like everyone else's timeline.

It did not fit neatly into four years.

But I made it.

And I need someone reading this to hear me clearly: Do not be discouraged if your climb is slow.

If you are working while studying—that is a hill.

If you are raising children while chasing a degree—that is a hill.

If you are carrying burdens nobody sees—that is a hill.

Slow progress is still progress.

Eventually, what once terrified me became something I could teach.

I taught my son.

I taught my daughter.

I even taught the neighborhood children how to drive a manual transmission.

They laugh now when they talk about those lessons.

They remember how serious I was.

How I made them practice balancing on a slope.

How I refused to let them panic when the car jerked or stalled.

Because I knew something they didn't yet understand.

If you can learn to drive a stick shift on a hill, you can handle life.

To this day, they thank me for those lessons.

But what they may not realize is that I was not just teaching them how to drive.

I was teaching them how to endure.

Hills will come.

Life will stall.

Dreams will jerk forward and then hesitate.

People will sit too close behind you.

Pressure will feel heavy.

But you must learn how to shift.

You must learn how to balance faith and effort.

You must learn how to trust that even if you roll back a little, you are not defeated.

Psalm 121 says, "I will lift up mine eyes unto the hills."

That scripture meant something different to me after driving that Ford Escort.

The hill was not my enemy.

It was my training ground.

And every time I made it to the top without stalling, I gained confidence that I could climb the next one too.

Life will stall.

Hills will come.

You will roll back sometimes.

But, honey baby child, you better know how to shift and move.

WHAT THIS MEANS FOR YOUR LIFE

I want to talk to the person reading this who feels behind.

Maybe you're watching your friends graduate while you're still working through prerequisites. Maybe you see people on social media buying homes while you're still renting. Maybe everyone around you seems to be climbing their hills effortlessly while you're stalling out, rolling backward, and praying nobody is watching.

I need you to hear this from a woman who took 10 years to do what others did in 4: **Slow progress is still progress.**

The world has sold us a lie that if it doesn't happen fast, it isn't happening. That if your timeline doesn't match the "normal" schedule, something is wrong with you. That urgency equals importance and speed equals success.

But the hill doesn't care how fast you climb it. The hill only cares that you don't stop.

Here is what my Ford Escort taught me about life:

First, you must learn how to balance pressure. The clutch and the gas pedal work against each other. Too much gas without enough clutch, and the car lurches forward dangerously. Too much clutch without enough gas, and you stall. Life works the same way. If you push too hard without pacing yourself, you burn out. If you hold back too much, you go nowhere. The rhythm is in the balance.

Second, rolling backward is not the same as failing. On that hill, I rolled back more times than I can count. But I never rolled all the way back to the bottom. I caught myself. I adjusted. I tried again. If you've lost ground—financially, relationally, academically, spiritually—you have not failed. You have rolled back. Now catch yourself and try again.

Third, the people behind you are not your enemy. I used to be terrified of the cars sitting too close behind me on that hill. I thought they were judging me. But most of them were just waiting. Some of them had been on that same hill before. Don't let the pressure of what you think people are thinking stop you from climbing.

Fourth, what you survive, you can teach. Once I mastered that hill, I turned around and taught every child in my neighborhood how to drive a stick shift. Your struggle has a student on the other side of it. Somebody is watching you climb right now, and your perseverance is giving them permission to keep going.

APPLY THIS

- **Name your hill.** What is the thing in your life right now that feels too steep? Write it down. Don't let it live unnamed in your mind where it can grow larger than it actually is.
- **Check your timeline shame.** Are you comparing your pace to someone else's? Their hill is not your hill. Their car is not your car. Their season is not your season.
- **Find your clutch-and-gas balance.** Where in your life are you pushing too hard? Where are you not pushing hard enough? Identify one area where you need to adjust your rhythm this week.
- **Look behind you.** Who is watching you climb? A child? A coworker? A friend? Reach out to them. Tell them about your hill. Your honesty might be the encouragement they need.

IF YOU'RE IN A GROUP

- What is a "hill" you are currently climbing that feels impossibly steep? How long have you been on it?
- Have you ever felt shame about your timeline? How has that shame affected your faith?
- Carolyn says, "If you can learn to drive a stick shift on a hill, you can handle life." What skill or lesson from your past prepared you for a challenge you didn't see coming?

Prayer: Father, I confess that I have been discouraged by my own pace. I have looked at other people's journeys and wondered why mine is taking so long. Remind me that You are not in a hurry, and that my timing is not a mistake. Give me the endurance to keep climbing when my legs are tired and the faith to trust that the top is closer than it feels. In Jesus's name. Amen.

"The hill is not there to stop you—it is there to teach you how to climb."

CHAPTER 3

DIVIDED HOUSES, SAME GOD

Written by Thoris Lamar Burt

"A father to the fatherless, a defender of widows, is God in his holy dwelling."

PSALM 68:5 (NIV)

Before trauma had a name in my life…

Before divorce redefined me…

Before November 26, 2023, tried to silence me in the garage…

There was a little boy in Alabama just trying to understand his place in the world.

I was raised by my single mama—alongside my sister Tracy and, later, my brother Terrell. I was the middle child. Not the firstborn who carries the initial expectations. Not the baby who receives the soft landing. The middle. The bridge. The quiet observer.

Mama was everything. Provider. Disciplinarian. Intercessor. Educator. Protector.

Every Saturday, without fail, we were in church. For Seventh-Day Adventists, Sabbath wasn't just a calendar mark—it was sacred ground. From sundown Friday to sundown Saturday, life slowed down. We ironed clothes on Friday nights. Shoes lined up by the door. Bibles ready.

Mama was a primary Sabbath School teacher. I remember sitting in her classroom when I was primary age, watching her teach with conviction. She didn't just teach memory verses—she taught identity. She taught that we belonged to God even if we didn't belong to a traditional family structure.

Faith became my first sense of stability.

But stability at home was layered.

My sister Tracy stayed with Gran Gran most of the time. As a child, I didn't understand why my sister slept in another house. I didn't understand why holidays and birthdays sometimes felt split. I just knew I missed her.

I would spend time at Gran Gran's house just to be close to Tracy. I didn't have language for it then, but I felt the separation deeply. It wasn't abandonment. It wasn't rejection. It was protection.

Mama later explained that when Tracy was a baby, Gran Gran kept her so she wouldn't be out in the cold while Mama worked and went to school. Mama was building a future, climbing that hill at Alabama

A&M University every day, working full time, raising children, and taking classes at night. It took her ten years to earn her bachelor's degree.

Ten years.

Most people quit in two.

Tracy grew comfortable in Gran Gran's home. That became her rhythm. Her normal. And even now, there is still tension surrounding that season. Not because there wasn't love—but because love sometimes makes complicated decisions.

Before Terrell was born, it was just Tracy and me navigating that world.

Mama's boyfriend at the time was a police officer at Alabama A&M University. For a season, he was the closest thing I had to a father figure. He represented authority. Order. Structure. I didn't realize it then, but little boys crave consistency. Even borrowed consistency.

I didn't meet my biological father until I was about 6 or 7 years old.

I don't remember the first private conversation. But I remember the van.

Burgundy and tan Ford conversion van.

It pulled into the projects like a symbol of another world. I remember feeling proud—like royalty had arrived for me.

Inside were siblings I had never met before: Jeremy, TJ, and Tina.

I was the oldest of his children.

That realization alone carried weight. I had been living one story, and suddenly I realized I was part of another one too.

When I went to his house for the first time, I remember looking around and thinking, *Wow… this is a house.*

Not the projects.

Not roaches scattering when the lights came on.

Not survival mode.

I saw clean carpet. Nice clothes. Matching sneakers. Gaming systems. Go-karts. Bicycles.

And I remember wondering—quietly—why my life looked different.

I never said it out loud. But comparison planted questions in my heart.

Were we less favored?

Were we less important?

Did God distribute blessings unevenly?

As a child, you don't articulate those thoughts. You absorb them.

But I loved being with my siblings. We were kids. We laughed. We rode bikes. We created memories that still make me smile.

One day, Jeremy asked a question that cut through innocence: "How do you have a different mother than we do?"

Silence followed.

I don't remember an answer being given. I just remember realizing that even children can sense complexity.

Visiting my father's Church of Christ introduced me to another spiritual rhythm. No instruments. No drums. No organ. Just harmonies rising from human lungs.

At first, it felt different from what I was used to. But over time, I realized something powerful: When voices blend without instruments, there's nowhere to hide. You either carry your part—or the harmony suffers.

Family is like that too.

Two churches.

Two households.

One same God.

The First Lady of that church later became my middle school guidance counselor. That wasn't coincidence. That was orchestration.

She poured into me academically, but she also reinforced something deeper—that I was not a fragmented child. I was not a divided identity. I was not a mistake navigating two households.

I was chosen.

Looking back now, I see things differently.

I see a single mother doing the best she could with limited resources but unlimited faith.

I see a grandmother stepping in out of protection, not interference.

I see a father trying to manage two worlds imperfectly.

I see siblings asking honest questions.

I see a little boy trying to make sense of it all.

And I see God.

God was in the projects.

God was in the van.

God was in the Sabbath School classroom.

God was in the acapella harmonies.

God was in the tension.

God was in the silence.

I didn't grow up with a traditional two-parent household. But I grew up with prayer covering me like insulation. I grew up watching a woman refuse to quit. I grew up knowing Scripture before I knew sociology.

And when later storms tried to take me out—when depression whispered lies, when divorce shook my foundation, when November 26 tried to write a final chapter—the faith planted in those early years rose up.

That's the part people don't always see.

Broken beginnings can produce unbreakable faith.

I am not the product of abandonment.

I am the product of endurance.

I am not divided.

I am layered.

And even in houses that felt split—God was building one continuous story.

WHAT THIS MEANS FOR YOUR LIFE

I need to talk to every child who grew up in two houses. Every son or daughter who spent holidays wondering which parent's table to sit at. Every kid who packed a bag on Fridays and unpacked it on Sundays. Every grown adult who still carries the quiet ache of feeling like they belonged everywhere and nowhere at the same time.

You are not divided. You are layered.

That distinction matters. Divided means broken into pieces that don't fit together. Layered means built with depth, complexity, and texture that a single-story life could never produce.

I want to name three wounds that children of divided houses carry into adulthood, because if you can name them, you can begin healing them:

The Wound of Comparison. I saw my father's house and immediately compared it to the projects. Clean carpet versus roaches. Go-karts versus survival. That comparison planted a question in my heart that took decades to uproot: "Am I less valuable?" If you grew up straddling two different economic realities, comparison may have convinced you that one side of your family loved you more—or that you were worth more on one side than the other. That is a lie. Your value was never determined by square footage.

The Wound of Silence. One day, my brother Jeremy asked a question that cut through innocence: "How do you have a different mother than we do?" Silence followed. Nobody explained it. Nobody processed it. Children in divided homes learn very early that some questions are not safe to ask. So, they stop asking. And the silence hardens into assumption. If you stopped asking questions as a child because the answers felt dangerous, I want to give you permission right now: Ask. Not to accuse. Not to punish. But to understand.

The Wound of Identity. When you live in two houses, you learn to code-switch. You learn which version of yourself is welcome at which table. Over time, you stop knowing which version is the real you. But here is the truth: Every version is real. You are not performing. You are adapting. And adaptation is not weakness—it is intelligence shaped by survival.

God was in both houses. God was in both churches. God was in the projects and in the conversion van. He does not pick sides in your family. He picks you.

APPLY THIS

- **Name which wound resonates most.** Comparison, silence, or identity? Write one sentence about how that wound has shown up in your adult life.
- **Write a letter to your childhood self.** Tell them what you wish someone had told you then. You don't need to send it to anyone. Just write it.
- **Identify one "First Lady" in your life.** Someone who poured into you when your home felt fractured. Thank them if you can. And if you can't, become that person for someone else.
- **Release the comparison.** If you still carry resentment about what one side of your family had versus the other, bring it to God in prayer this week. Comparison is a thief. It steals gratitude. Let it go.

IF YOU'RE IN A GROUP

- Did you grow up navigating two households? What was the hardest part that nobody talked about?
- Thoris says, "As a child, you don't articulate those thoughts. You absorb them." What is something you absorbed as a child that you're only now recognizing?
- How has your experience of a divided or non-traditional family shaped your faith—positively or negatively?

Prayer: Father God, thank you for covering me in seasons I didn't understand. Thank you for being Father where there were gaps. Heal every lingering tension in my family story. Redeem what felt divided.

Help me carry both sides of my identity with grace and without resentment. You were present in every house I entered. And You are still present now. Amen.

"Broken beginnings can produce unbreakable faith."

CHAPTER 4

SEEDS OF RESPONSIBILITY–CREDIT, CARS, AND CALLING

Written by Thoris Lamar Burt

"Train up a child in the way he should go: and when he is old, he will not depart from it."

PROVERBS 22:6

My mama taught me financial literacy when I was fourteen years old.

Fourteen.

I was living in Huntsville, Alabama, where I landed my first job with the federal government working at the NCO Club on Redstone Arsenal as a food service worker (aka a dishwasher). Later that year, we relocated to Orlando, Florida, and that's when I started working at Publix Supermarkets as a front service worker (aka a bag boy).

Most boys that age are thinking about sneakers, video games, or trying to impress girls. I was being taught about credit scores, interest rates, and long-term responsibility. At the time, I didn't realize how rare that was.

Mama told me plainly, "Son, if you want a car, you need to save for it."

So, I did.

I worked summer jobs. I did odd chores. I stacked every dollar I could. I denied myself small pleasures because I had a bigger goal in mind. I wasn't just saving for a car—I was learning delayed gratification.

When the day finally came and I had enough saved, I thought I would walk onto the lot and pay cash outright. I felt proud. Independent. Self-made.

But Mama had another plan tucked quietly in her back pocket.

She said, "No. We're going to build your credit."

I didn't fully understand what that meant. I thought paying cash was the smartest move. No debt. No payments. Clean and simple.

But she saw further than I did.

Instead of paying upfront, she co-signed an auto loan so I could establish a credit history. She intentionally chose structure over convenience. She understood something I didn't yet grasp—that credit is not about buying things; it's about building access.

That was my first real lesson in stewardship.

Paying bills on time wasn't about the car.

It wasn't about appearances.

It was about discipline.

It was about proving that I could be trusted with responsibility.

Every payment I made was a promise kept.

Every on-time installment was character reinforced.

By the time I was eighteen, that small decision had grown into something powerful. My credit score hit 800—not because I had wealth, but because I had consistency.

That discipline opened doors.

Credit cards with favorable limits.

Better interest rates.

Opportunities to leverage capital.

Eventually, the ability to purchase my first home.

But here's what I understand now that I didn't understand then: Mama wasn't just building my credit score. She was building my confidence. She was teaching me that responsibility precedes authority.

That discipline unlocks freedom.

That preparation creates opportunity.

Those early seeds became part of my calling.

Because stewardship is spiritual.

When God gives you something—whether it's money, talent, influence, or opportunity—how you manage it determines what He trusts you with next.

Responsibility grows quietly.

It doesn't announce itself.

It doesn't brag.

It compounds.

And let me say this plainly to parents reading this: You have even more tools today than my mama had back then. You can add your child as an authorized user on a well-established credit card. You can allow them to inherit positive credit age, strong payment history, and healthy reporting long before they ever turn eighteen.

But let's keep it real.

If your credit is raggedy—late payments, high balances, poor history—do not pass that down. That is not generational wealth; that is generational burden.

The goal is to set them up, not set them back.

Financial literacy is not about materialism; it is about protection. It protects your children from predatory interest rates. It protects them from financial desperation. It protects their future borrowing power.

Teach them early.

Show them statements. Explain interest. Break down how minimum payments trap people. Model consistency.

Because children don't just listen to what you say. They absorb what you demonstrate.

When I look back at fourteen-year-old me, I see a boy learning something far deeper than money management. I was learning identity. I was learning that I was capable. That I could build something stable. That discipline was not punishment—it was power.

And that lesson carried into everything else in my life.

Into sales quotas. Into saving for a home. Into managing risk. Into navigating setbacks.

Responsibility planted roots. Discipline strengthened them.

And over time, those roots held me steady when storms came.

Financial literacy isn't flashy. It doesn't trend on social media. It doesn't get applause. But it builds infrastructure. And infrastructure is what allows dreams to stand.

My mama planted seeds when I was fourteen. She didn't just give me a car. She gave me a framework. And that framework became part of my calling.

Because what you honor early becomes the harvest you live on later.

WHAT THIS MEANS FOR YOUR LIFE

This is the chapter where I need to stop telling my story and start talking to parents.

If you have children, teenagers, or young adults in your home, I want you to hear me clearly: **Financial literacy is not optional; it is protection.**

My mama gave me something at fourteen that many adults still don't have: a working understanding of how credit, debt, and money actually function. She didn't just hand me principles. She gave me practice. She made me save, then she didn't let me spend it all at once. She co-signed a loan not because I couldn't afford the car, but because she was playing a longer game.

That longer game is what separates parents who give their children things from parents who give their children tools.

Here is what I want every parent, guardian, and mentor reading this to know:

You can start building your child's credit before they turn eighteen. Add them as an authorized user on a well-established credit card—one with a strong payment history, low balance-to-limit ratio, and years of age. When you do this, that card's positive history begins reporting on your child's credit file. By the time they turn eighteen, they could already have years of credit history before they ever apply for a single thing on their own.

But here is the warning: If your credit is unhealthy—late payments, high balances, collections—do not pass that down. That is not generational wealth; that is generational burden. Fix yours first. Then extend the blessing.

Four principles my mama modeled that I now pass on to you:

Principle 1: Teach saving before spending. Before my mama let me think about what I wanted to buy, she taught me to save for it first. This builds delayed gratification—the single most important financial skill a young person can develop.

Principle 2: Teach credit before debt. Most people learn about debt the hard way—through interest, fees, and buried balances. My mama taught me credit as a tool for building access, not as a shortcut for buying things I couldn't afford.

Principle 3: Teach consistency over windfalls. My credit score didn't hit 800 because of one big payment. It hit 800 because of small, consistent, on-time payments made month after month. Faithfulness in small things leads to authority over larger things (Luke 16:10).

Principle 4: Teach stewardship as worship. Money is not the goal; management is. When God gives you something—whether it's money, talent, influence, or opportunity—how you manage it determines what He trusts you with next.

APPLY THIS

- **If you have children under eighteen:** Research adding them as an authorized user on your strongest credit card this week.

- **If your own credit needs repair:** Commit to one action this month that improves your own financial health—whether that's disputing an error, paying down a balance, or setting up autopay.
- **Have "the money talk" this week.** Sit down with a young person in your life and explain one financial concept: credit scores, interest rates, or the difference between needs and wants.
- **Model what you teach.** Let your children see you pay bills. Let them see the budget. Children don't just listen to what you say—they absorb what you demonstrate.

IF YOU'RE IN A GROUP

- At what age did you first learn about credit or money management? Was it from a parent, a mentor, or the hard way?
- Thoris's mama chose to co-sign a loan instead of letting him pay cash. Do you agree with that decision? Why or why not?
- How does the idea of "stewardship as worship" change the way you think about money?

Prayer: Father God, thank you for the seeds of responsibility planted in me when I was too young to understand their value. Teach me to plant those same seeds in the next generation. Give me wisdom with what You've entrusted to me—time, talent, and treasure. Help me model consistency, discipline, and stewardship so that what I build today becomes the harvest someone else lives on tomorrow. In Jesus's name, Amen.

"Responsibility grows roots, but discipline makes them strong. What you honor early becomes the harvest you live on later."

PART II

RISING: WHEN PURPOSE MEETS PRESSURE

Core Teaching: God doesn't cancel the dream. He engineers a different version of it.

CHAPTER 5

ENGINEERING DREAMS AND DETOURS

Written by Thoris Lamar Burt

"In their hearts humans plan their course, but the Lord establishes their steps."

PROVERBS 16:9 (NIV)

After my Uncle Don's suicide in 1996, life did not slow down long enough for me to process anything.

I graduated from University High School in May of 1995. I walked across that stage not knowing the grief or the ambition I would soon experience—a grief I would not know how to name and an ambition I would not know how to steward.

People often ask me, "Did you go to college?"

Yes.

But the real answer is: I wrestled with college.

In middle school and high school, I fell in love with Hondas. The thoughtful kind. The intentional design. The way the interior wrapped around the driver. The ergonomic placement of every button and dial. I would sit in the driver's seat and analyze everything—the curvature of the dashboard, the angle of the steering wheel, the placement of the gear shift.

I didn't just see a car.

I saw systems.

I saw design.

I saw order.

That is how I decided I wanted to become an industrial engineer.

I dreamed of working in Honda's Research & Development department, designing ergonomic systems that improved human interaction with machines. I imagined myself in a lab coat, drafting designs and optimizing processes.

It felt purposeful.

Because my father is a veteran of the United States Army, I had the opportunity to attend any Alabama state college tuition-free.

Free.

That word echoed in my mind like destiny knocking.

I applied and was accepted to the University of Alabama in Huntsville, College of Engineering. I toured the campus. I imagined dorm life. I imagined independence. I imagined redemption before an unforeseeable loss.

But my mother forbade me from attending.

She was concerned that returning to Huntsville would reconnect me with two cousins who were entangled in the wrong crowd. She feared I would be pulled into something that would derail my future.

I was angry.

I did not understand how she could block a free education—an engineering degree—over fear of association.

It felt unfair.

It felt controlling.

It felt like she did not trust me.

That decision left a mark.

College no longer felt like an opportunity—it felt like compromise. And now, I had to pay for it.

In hindsight, my mother's instinct was right. The two cousins she feared would influence me are both incarcerated and have been for decades.

What I saw as restriction was protection.

But protection does not always feel kind in the moment.

After wrestling with disappointment, I enrolled in summer classes at Valencia Community College East. It felt like a consolation prize. In the fall, I began attending the University of Central Florida.

I pursued industrial engineering.

One of my favorite classes was Intro to Industrial Engineering taught by Dr. Pamela McCauley. I loved her class. I was engaged. I earned an *A*. For the first time since high school, I felt aligned again with that teenage dream of designing systems.

But then physics entered the chat.

Then calculus.

Those classes did not just challenge me—they humbled me. No matter how much time I studied, the formulas refused to click. The equations blurred. The exams exposed gaps in my foundation.

Eventually, I failed.

Failing those classes felt like failing myself.

It wasn't just academic.

It was identity.

If I was not going to be an engineer, then who was I?

That is when I pivoted to business management.

Around the same time, I was still working at Publix. Shortly after, I began working at AT&T, and the money I started earning at AT&T

was hovering near the salary of an entry-level engineer. That reality began shifting my motivation.

Why fight through calculus when I was already earning what engineers earned? Why endure academic frustration when sales felt natural? The more money I made, the less I wanted to attend class. I was forcing myself to stay enrolled because it mattered to my mother. Education was sacred to her, but resentment began building inside me.

I remember report cards approaching. My GPA hovered around a 2.0—maybe lower. I knew a guy at UCF who had a reputation for manipulating grades. I considered it; that alone tells you how far my heart had drifted from purpose. My mother found out. I do not remember the exact details of how she discovered it, but she did. And when she confronted me, I did not lie. I was brutally honest. I told her I hated school. I told her I no longer wanted to go. I told her I was happy making money. I told her I felt successful already.

She was disappointed, and disappointment from your mother hits differently than any failed exam, but, still, I stepped fully into sales.

Because at twenty-one years old, I was making more money than my mother was making with a college degree.

That fact shaped my ego. It shaped my confidence. It shaped my decisions. It reinforced the belief that I did not need a degree to succeed.

In 2000, I attempted to return to school through the University of Phoenix. My employer offered onsite evening classes that were fully paid. I took management courses and performed well.

It felt redemptive.

But then the office closed. Another interruption. Another detour.

In 2006, I tried again. I enrolled in more courses at the University of Phoenix. But life, ambition, and career momentum pulled me in other directions.

I never completed my bachelor's degree.

For years, that felt like an unfinished sentence in my life story. It felt like something missing. Something incomplete. Something I should have conquered.

But over time, I began to see something differently. The engineering mindset never left me. I did not design dashboards—I designed sales processes. I did not optimize production lines—I optimized pipelines. I did not work in R&D labs—I worked in revenue development.

The systems thinking remained. God did not discard the gift; He redirected it.

Proverbs 16:9 says we plan our course, but the Lord establishes our steps.

My course said engineer.

God's steps said salesman, strategist, communicator.

And if I am honest, my sales career required the same discipline, the same analysis, the same optimization mindset I once admired in Honda's ergonomic designs.

The degree was unfinished, but the design was not.

Looking back now, I see that the disappointment of not attending University of Alabama in Huntsville protected me. The failure in calculus humbled me. The pivot to business prepared me. The success in sales affirmed me.

Sometimes God does not cancel the dream. He engineers a different version of it.

WHAT THIS MEANS FOR YOUR LIFE

I want to talk to two types of people right now.

First: the person who was stopped from pursuing their dream by someone they love. Maybe a parent blocked a college choice. Maybe a spouse discouraged a career move. Maybe a pastor steered you away from a calling they didn't understand. And you've been carrying resentment about it ever since.

I need you to consider the possibility that what felt like sabotage was actually salvation. Not always. Not automatically. But sometimes the people who love you can see dangers you can't. My mother's "no" felt like control; it was protection. Two decades later, the evidence confirmed what her instinct already knew.

This does not mean every "no" from a loved one is God speaking. Discernment matters. But before you build a monument to your resentment, ask God honestly: "Was there protection in that redirection?"

Second: the person who pivoted from their original dream and still feels like they failed. You started as pre-med and ended up in teaching. You wanted to be a lawyer and became a nonprofit director. You dreamed of engineering and ended up in sales.

Here is what Proverbs 16:9 is really saying: **God is not reckless with your gifts. He is strategic with them.**

My engineering mind didn't die when I left UCF. It expressed itself differently. The same analytical thinking, the same systems orientation, the same love of optimization—it all transferred. God didn't waste the dream. He gave it a different address.

Your original dream was not wasted either. The skills you developed pursuing it, the discipline you built, the passion you cultivated—those are transferable. God doesn't throw away blueprints; He revises them.

The question is not "Did I fail?" The question is "Where did the gift land?"

APPLY THIS

- **Trace the transfer.** Write down the skills or passions from your original dream. Now identify where those same skills show up in your current life or career. The gift didn't die. It migrated.
- **Release the resentment.** If someone you love redirected your path and you've been angry about it, bring that anger to God this week. Ask Him to show you what He was protecting you from—or preparing you for.

- **Stop calling your pivot a failure.** A pivot is not a failure. It is a recalculation. Rename your "failure" today. Call it what it actually was: a redirection.
- **If you have a child facing a detour:** Don't dismiss their grief. When a young person's dream changes course, they're not just losing a plan—they're losing an identity. Validate the pain before you offer the lesson.

IF YOU'RE IN A GROUP

- Have you ever been blocked from something you wanted—and later realized it was protection?
- Thoris says his engineering mind didn't die; it just found a different address. Where do you see your original passions living in your current life?
- How do you distinguish between God redirecting you and you simply giving up?

Prayer: Father God, thank you for protecting me from paths that were not meant for me. Thank you for allowing disappointment to refine me rather than define me. Help me see every detour as divine engineering. Continue establishing my steps, even when my plans shift. In Jesus's name. Amen.

"The blueprint changed,

but the Builder never did."

CHAPTER 6

A FATHER'S LOVE, AN UNCLE'S DEATH

Written by Thoris Lamar Burt

"There is a time for everything, and a season for every activity under the heavens: a time to be born and a time to die..."

ECCLESIASTES 3:1-2 (NIV)

Life has a strange way of circling back on itself—like it's trying to teach you something you didn't have the language for yet. It revisits you in echoes. In memories. In patterns you swore you would never repeat. Sometimes it doesn't come as a lesson. Sometimes it comes as a warning you only recognize in hindsight.

My father, Thomas Lee Malone, came from a big Alabama family. Eight brothers and six sisters. Fourteen branches on one tree. In a family that large, it's easy to disappear. Easy to become an afterthought. Easy to be the child that people say they'll check on but never do. So, when I arrived in this world, there was only one uncle from that entire limb who chose to reach for me. Only one who thought I mattered enough to show up.

That was my Uncle Don.

He didn't just carry the Malone name—he carried heart. He'd come by to see me when I was little, to talk to me like I was somebody, and to slip my mama a few dollars to help buy me the things I needed. He didn't have a lot, but what he did have, he shared. Quietly. Generously. Consistently.

Uncle Don didn't announce it. He didn't brag about it. He just showed up. He was the only one on my father's side who treated me like kin. And when you grow up feeling half-connected to one side of your family, that kind of presence means everything. It makes you feel claimed. It makes you feel chosen.

That's why his death in 1996, when I was just 18 years old, shattered me in a way I didn't know how to process. I had just graduated high school the year before. I was standing at the doorway of adulthood when the news hit that my Uncle Don had taken his own life.

Eighteen is old enough to understand death.

But not old enough to understand despair.

I remember exactly where I was when the words reached me.

I remember the way the air left my body.

I remember the ache in my chest that didn't know where to go.

Grief at that age doesn't come with vocabulary; it comes with silence. With questions you don't ask out loud. With a heaviness that follows you into quiet rooms.

To lose the one person from that side of my family who ever made the effort to love me—and to lose him to suicide—cut deep in a place I didn't have the tools to understand at eighteen. It was grief, confusion, abandonment, and shock all braided together.

And underneath it all was a question I never voiced: Why didn't he stay?

What I didn't know back then was that the same darkness that swallowed him ... would one day come for me.

Not immediately. Not dramatically. But slowly. Subtly. Patiently.

Nearly twenty-seven years later, I found myself in my own garage, fighting for my life in the same kind of storm. I believed the same lie he did—that maybe the world would be better off without me. That maybe my death would be more valuable than my life. That the people I loved would hurt less if I just ... disappeared.

Depression doesn't create new lies.

It recycles old ones.

And somewhere in the unseen realm, it felt like history was trying to repeat itself.

But here's the part that shows the fingerprints of God: I survived the thing that took Uncle Don. The enemy tried to recycle that generational spirit of despair, to run the same play twice in the same bloodline—but God stopped the cycle with me.

That realization still humbles me. Because survival is not superiority; it's mercy.

When I think about Uncle Don now, I don't just think about his death. I think about his love. His effort. His generosity. His way of seeing me when others didn't bother. I think about how he sowed into my life when I was too young to understand how rare that kind of care was. I think about the small bills he slipped into my mama's hand. The conversations he had with me like I mattered. The way he chose presence over distance.

Uncle Don didn't get to finish his story.

But God kept me long enough to finish mine—and to tell his. That is not something I take lightly.

His life and loss are part of the reason I fight to stay here. Part of the reason I talk about mental health out loud instead of hiding it. Part of the reason this book exists at all.

Because silence almost killed us.

Because pretending almost erased us.

Because pride almost buried us.

Because when I say, "Why HE kept me," I'm not just talking about God keeping my heart beating. I'm talking about Him giving me the strength to break cycles my family couldn't break before me—cycles of silence, shame, and suicide.

I am not just living for myself. I am living as interruption.

And in that way, a Father's love and an uncle's death both became part of my survival story.

WHAT THIS MEANS FOR YOUR LIFE

I want to name something the church has been afraid to talk about for too long: **Suicide runs in families. Not because it's genetic. Because silence is.**

My Uncle Don took his life in 1996. Nearly twenty-seven years later, I found myself in my own garage fighting the same battle. The enemy didn't create a new playbook; he recycled the old one. Same bloodline. Same lie. Same darkness.

Here is what I need you to understand: When a family member dies by suicide and nobody talks about it—nobody processes it, nobody names the grief, nobody addresses the mental health patterns that led to it—that silence becomes a seed. It drops into the soil of the next generation and waits.

Depression doesn't create new lies; it recycles old ones.

If there is a history of suicide, depression, or mental illness in your family, and you have never talked about it openly, I am asking you—I am begging you—to break that silence. Not for your sake alone. For the person in your bloodline who is carrying a weight they cannot name because nobody ever gave it a name.

Three truths about generational patterns of despair:

The pattern is not your destiny: Just because someone in your family lost their battle does not mean you will lose yours. I survived the thing that took my uncle. The cycle can stop with you, but you have to be intentional about stopping it.

Survival is not superiority—it is mercy: I am not stronger than Uncle Don. I am not better. I am not more faithful. I was simply interrupted by grace. If you survived what someone else in your family did not, do not carry survivor's guilt. Carry purpose.

Talking about it is the first act of healing: If your family has a history of mental health struggles, say it out loud. In your home. In your church. In your therapy sessions. Silence protects stigma. Truth protects lives.

APPLY THIS

- **Ask the family question.** Is there a history of depression, anxiety, or suicide in your family that has never been openly discussed? Just ask: "Did anyone in our family ever struggle with their mental health?"
- **Break one silence this week.** Tell one trusted person about something you've been carrying alone. A counselor. A friend. A pastor. Just one person.
- **If you have lost someone to suicide:** You are not responsible for their decision. You could not have saved them by loving them harder. Grief is yours to carry; guilt is not.

IF YOU'RE IN A GROUP

- Has mental health ever been discussed openly in your family? Why or why not?
- Thoris says, "Depression doesn't create new lies—it recycles old ones." What old lies have you recognized in your own family history?

- How can the church better address generational patterns of mental illness without stigma?

Prayer: Father God, break every generational cycle of silence, shame, and despair in my bloodline. Where the enemy has recycled old lies, speak new truth. Where death has stolen, let life interrupt. Give me the courage to say out loud what my family has been afraid to whisper. In Jesus's name. Amen.

"Some family stories wound you.

Others warn you.

But the ones God redeems…

those are the stories that save you."

CHAPTER 7

WHEN MAMA STOPS BELIEVING IN YOU

Written by Thoris Lamar Burt

"Can a mother forget the baby at her breast and have no compassion on the child she has borne? Though she may forget, I will not forget you!"

ISAIAH 49:15 (NIV)

There were moments in my life when my mama stopped believing in me—not because she didn't love me, but because life had handed us a string of misunderstandings, fears, and bad timing that clouded the truth.

And when I say she stopped believing in me, I don't mean she stopped loving me. I mean I could see it in her eyes—the hesitation, the questioning, the guarded tone. The shift. The kind of shift that makes you realize trust has been bruised and something sacred feels fragile.

The first time was years earlier—long before any surgery, any diagnosis, any hospital stay. I moved money out of her account to pay for my car after losing my job. I wasn't trying to hurt her: I was young, stressed, and thought I could fix it before she noticed. When she confronted me, the shame hit me hard. I told her I would pay it back—and I did—but the trust had already been shaken.

What she saw was betrayal. What I felt was desperation. I thought I was buying time; she thought I was breaking covenant. That moment sat heavy between us. Even after repayment, the emotional balance sheet still showed a deficit. Trust, once cracked, doesn't snap back instantly—it has to be rebuilt, plank by plank.

The second time was over a credit card. One was in her name, but she later discovered she'd been added as an authorized user to my account. She thought the whole thing had been set up under her name. Miscommunication turned into disappointment.

And disappointment is quiet. It doesn't scream. It settles. It lingers. It changes how conversations sound. That situation wasn't about fraud—it was about perception. And perception can wound just as deeply as truth. It created distance where clarity should have lived.

The third moment cut even deeper—and this one came decades later, in 2024. After her major surgery, she believed I had moved thousands of dollars out of her account. She didn't remember that she had transferred the funds to me for her home accessibility upgrades—because the anesthesia had affected her memory. She thought I had taken advantage of her at the most vulnerable point in her life—that broke me.

It didn't just hurt—it shattered something inside of me. To be seen as a thief when you are serving. To be seen as opportunistic when you are sacrificing. I was the one arranging contractors. I was the one making sure her home would be safe for her recovery. But in her mind, I had become someone else. And there is no pain quite like being misidentified by the person who knows you best.

The fourth time came when she couldn't find her laptop. I was the only one who had been in the house, and she asked me where it was. I truly hadn't seen it. She was convinced I had taken it—until her friend, helping her pack for a Boston trip, found it tucked inside her large suitcase.

Again, silence followed. No grand apology. Just the quiet undoing of suspicion. But even when accusations are resolved, the echo of them lingers.

And then, the house keys went missing. Again, I was the only one around. Again, she thought I had them. But later, she found them in my old bedroom—the very room she sleeps in sometimes.

Each accusation may have seemed small individually. But together, they built a narrative I never wanted attached to my name. A pattern I never authored.

Each moment added a crack, not just in her trust but in my spirit. Because nothing hurts like being seen as the villain when your heart knows you're trying to help.

It makes you question yourself. It makes you question how you're perceived. It makes you wonder if your efforts are invisible. It makes you wrestle silently with God, asking, "Why does this keep happening?"

But here's the truth my mama and I both had to learn:

Even when trust wavers, love doesn't die. Even when the mind forgets, the heart remembers. And even when a mother stops believing for a moment… God never does.

God sees intention when others see suspicion. God sees sacrifice when others see strategy. God sees service when others see selfishness.

And my mama—through every misunderstanding, every fear, every memory lapse, every tear—still stands on this truth:

"I will never stop believing in my children."

Because belief is not the absence of doubt. It is the decision to return to love after doubt tries to settle in.

And what we discovered is this:

Relationships bend under pressure. Memory can falter. Fear can distort. Pain can accuse.

But love—real love—has a way of finding the truth and stitching the broken pieces back together.

WHAT THIS MEANS FOR YOUR LIFE

There is a specific kind of pain that only comes from being misidentified by someone who is supposed to know you best. Not a stranger's accusation—that stings but heals quickly. This is the wound of being seen as a villain by the person who raised you, loved you, and should know your heart better than anyone.

If you have ever been accused of something by someone you love—and you were innocent—this chapter is for you.

Here are three things I've learned about surviving accusations from those closest to you:

First: their accusation is often about their pain, not your character. When my mama accused me of taking her money, it wasn't because she believed I was a thief in her heart. It was because anesthesia affected her memory, fear made her vulnerable, and confusion filled in the blanks with the worst possible explanation. Hurt people see threats where there are none.

Second: defending yourself is important, but not at the cost of the relationship. I could have walked away. I could have let bitterness build a wall. Instead, I chose to keep showing up—even when showing up meant being suspected. The relationship mattered more than being right.

Third: trust broken by misunderstanding can be rebuilt—but it requires both sides. Trust doesn't snap back; it's rebuilt plank by plank. If someone has lost faith in you unfairly, the path back is not argument. It's consistent, quiet evidence of who you actually are. Over time, truth outlasts suspicion.

APPLY THIS

- Is there someone in your life who has misidentified you? Write down what they believe about you versus what is true about you.

- Ask yourself honestly: "Am I protecting this relationship, or am I protecting my pride?"
- Pray for the person who misjudged you—not just for reconciliation, but for their healing. Their accusation likely came from their own unprocessed pain.

IF YOU'RE IN A GROUP

- Have you ever been accused of something by someone who loves you? How did it affect your relationship?
- Thoris says, "There is no pain quite like being misidentified by the person who knows you best." Do you agree? Why or why not?
- How do you rebuild trust after it's been damaged by misunderstanding rather than malice?

Prayer: Father God, heal every wound caused by being misidentified by someone I love. Where suspicion has stolen trust, restore it through quiet faithfulness. Where hurt has built walls, give me the patience to dismantle them, one act of love at a time. Remind me that the relationship matters more than being right, and that truth outlasts every accusation. In Jesus's name. Amen.

"Being misidentified by someone who knows you is one of the deepest wounds. But God always restores what suspicion tries to steal."

CHAPTER 8

FROM STRIP CLUBS TO SPIRITUAL CLARITY

Written by Thoris Lamar Burt

"Therefore, if anyone is in Christ, the new creation has come: The old has gone, the new is here!"

2 CORINTHIANS 5:17 (NIV)

There was a season in my life when I was a road warrior—traveling from Orlando to West Palm Beach to Fort Lauderdale to Miami to Jacksonville to Atlanta, two weeks out of every month.

Airports became normal. Hotel rooms became temporary homes. Rental cars became confession booths where I sat alone with my thoughts longer than I should have. Movement was constant; accountability was not.

It wasn't a season I'm proud of, but it's part of my truth.

And the truth doesn't lose its power just because it makes you uncomfortable. Some chapters embarrass you. Some expose you. But if you don't name them, they keep naming you.

Growing up in the church, I had a strong foundation. I loved God. I didn't smoke, didn't drink, didn't do drugs—but sin doesn't need a substance. Sometimes it just needs a weakness. And weakness doesn't always look wild. Sometimes it looks successful. Sometimes it wears a suit and travels for business. Sometimes it hides behind ambition.

And mine? It was a habit that spiraled into a stronghold—a lifestyle that eventually cost me my marriage and my family. What started as curiosity became ritual. What started as occasional became patterned. What started as secrecy became double living.

On the road, the company paid for everything: hotels, rental cars, flights, food—and I was making great money with more disposable income than I'd ever had. Money without discipline magnifies character; it reveals what you worship when no one is watching.

Before marriage, my wife and I already operated like we were married. She worked out of state and sent me money to save for our future. Sometimes I saved it; sometimes I didn't. Sometimes I spent what she worked for on nonsense.

And that is a harder confession than the clubs themselves—because betrayal is not just physical. It's financial. It's emotional. It's spiritual.

After marriage, I thought I could turn it all off. But addiction doesn't bow to logic. Temptation doesn't obey vows. Cycles don't break because you "meant well."

Marriage exposed what I never confronted. I had long stretches where I stayed away. Moments where I really believed I was healed. But the urge would creep back in—quietly, strategically, in moments of stress, weakness, or loneliness. Addiction rarely screams; it whispers.

It tells you that you deserve an escape. It tells you that you're in control. It tells you that this will be the last time.

And each time, the line between habit and identity blurred a little more. Eventually, I was labeled a sex addict—a title that felt like chains and shame tied together.

Labels can imprison you if you let them. They can become prophecy if you accept them without a fight. For a long time, that label felt heavier than the sin itself. Because shame isolates. Shame convinces you that you are the only one fighting this battle. Shame convinces you that if people really knew you, they would walk away.

And in some cases, they did.

And there are so many scenarios where I know I should NOT be alive today. But God kept me. He kept me from violence. He kept me from diseases. He kept me from decisions that would have destroyed everything beyond repair. He kept me when my own willpower failed.

I'm not sharing this chapter to glorify the darkness—I'm sharing it because someone reading this thinks they've gone too far or messed up too badly.

You haven't.

You are not your lowest night.

You are not your secret struggle.

You are not your worst pattern.

I'm living proof that God can pull a man out of places he thought he loved and deliver him into a purpose he never imagined. Deliverance did not happen overnight. The old me died in stages, the new me grew in pieces, and both were necessary for God to rebuild me into who I am now.

Transformation is not clean. It is not instant. It is not glamorous. It is layered. It is humbling. It is costly.

And sometimes you don't even realize you've changed until you look back at who you used to be and realize that version of you would no longer feel comfortable in your current convictions.

Grace didn't excuse me. Grace confronted me. Grace exposed me. Grace rebuilt me.

And the clarity I have now did not come from pretending that season didn't exist—it came from owning it, repenting of it, and allowing God to redeem it.

The road warrior eventually found stillness. The double life eventually met truth. The stronghold eventually met surrender.

And surrender is where clarity begins.

WHAT THIS MEANS FOR YOUR LIFE

I am going to say something that might offend religious people but will liberate honest ones: **The church has become more comfortable with the appearance of purity than the process of deliverance.**

We celebrate the testimony but avoid the territory. We applaud the "I used to" while shaming the "I still struggle." And that hypocrisy is killing people in silence.

If you are reading this and you are in a battle with a stronghold—pornography, adultery, gambling, substances, emotional affairs, compulsive behavior—I need you to hear three truths:

Truth 1: Addiction doesn't bow to willpower. You cannot "try harder" your way out of a stronghold. Strongholds are not discipline problems. They are spiritual and neurological patterns that require intervention: therapy, accountability, confession, and often professional help. Willpower is not a weapon. It is a flashlight. It shows you the problem; it doesn't fix it.

Truth 2: Labels can imprison you if you let them. I was labeled a sex addict; that label felt like chains. For a long time, I became the label. But a label is a diagnosis, not a destiny. Don't let what you've been called become what you believe you are. You are not your pattern. You are a person with a pattern—and patterns can be broken.

Truth 3: Grace didn't excuse me. Grace confronted me. People misunderstand grace. They think grace means God overlooks sin. Grace doesn't overlook—it overhauls. Grace exposed me. Grace humbled me. Grace rebuilt me. Grace is not permission to stay the same. Grace is power to become someone new.

APPLY THIS

- Name your stronghold—to yourself and to one trusted person. Shame grows in secrecy. It shrinks in the light.

- Stop fighting alone. Find a counselor, an accountability partner, or a support group. Isolation is the stronghold's greatest ally.
- Separate your identity from your pattern. You are not your worst night. Say it out loud.

IF YOU'RE IN A GROUP

- How does the church typically respond to members who confess ongoing struggles with addiction or sexual sin? How should it respond?
- Thoris says, "Grace didn't excuse me—grace confronted me." How does that reframe your understanding of grace?
- What is the difference between a habit and a stronghold? How do you know when you've crossed the line?

Prayer: Father God, I confess that I have fought battles in secret that I should have brought into the light. Break every stronghold that has made its home in my life. Replace shame with honesty. Replace isolation with community. Replace the label with my true identity in You. In Jesus's name. Amen.

"Grace doesn't erase your past—it transforms who you become after it."

PART III

COVENANT: LOVE, LOSS, AND LETTING GO

Core Teaching: Love is not the absence of struggle—it is the decision to stay sacred in the middle of it.

CHAPTER 9

THE DAY I MARRIED MY BEST FRIEND

Written by Thoris Lamar Burt

"He who finds a wife finds what is good and receives favor from the Lord."

PROVERBS 18:22 (NIV)

August 17, 2007, was a Friday. Sunny. Clear. Beautiful in a way that almost felt symbolic.

But that day didn't start at the altar. It started long before—on highways, in long-distance calls, in sacrifice, in growth, and in a decision to choose covenant over chaos.

The year before we got married, my wife was living in Connecticut, working as a nanny for a very wealthy family. She had been there for years—stable, secure, and trusted. She helped raise children that weren't hers. She sacrificed pieces of herself for other people's families while we were still building ours from a distance.

There's something humbling about watching someone nurture other people's futures while you're still trying to build your own. And I knew something. If we were going to build a future, I had to move her back to Orlando.

So, I rented a U-Haul truck and set out on that journey—not just to move furniture, but to move destiny.

My future wife didn't come alone. One of her nieces—just four years old at the time—came with her; that little girl would later become a major part of our lives. But in that moment, I wasn't just moving my girlfriend home. I was stepping into responsibility.

I wasn't just bringing her back to Florida. I was saying, "I am ready to lead."

I remember something most people would overlook. Back then, cell phones had roaming charges once you left your local coverage area or state. And if you weren't careful, a long-distance call could cost you a small fortune. But I had worked at AT&T, and I knew something most people didn't. If you initiated the call inside your local coverage area—and the call never disconnected—you wouldn't be charged roaming, no matter how far you drove.

So the day I left Orlando to drive north, I called her before I crossed state lines. And we stayed on the phone. The entire time. From Orlando to Alexandria, Virginia—where I stopped to rest at a friend's house—the call never dropped. Not once. No static. No interruptions. No disconnections.

Twelve hours, 31 minutes, and 59 seconds. And not one dropped call.

It felt divine. It felt ordained. It felt like God was saying, "This connection is covered."

For twelve hours, we talked about everything. Our love. Our plans. Getting engaged. Getting married. Buying our first home. Starting a family.

We dreamed out loud.

We spoke our future into existence across state lines and open highways.

And I remember thinking—this is not normal. No dropped call. No signal fade. No roaming charge. Just clarity. That call was free of charge.

But it cost me something. It cost pride. It cost selfishness. It cost the old habits I was trying to leave behind. Because loving her meant becoming someone better.

After the season I described in the last chapter—the road warrior life, the temptations, the cycles—marriage was not just romance. It was repentance. It was growth. It was me saying, "I choose covenant over comfort."

When she finally moved back to Orlando, and we began planning our engagement and wedding, something inside me felt different. Not perfect. Not fully healed. But intentional.

August 17, 2007, arrived.

It was a beautiful, sunny Friday.

But before we stood in front of anyone, we made a decision that only the two of us fully understood. We drove to Titusville, Florida. Not because it was glamorous. Not because it was our dream destination.

But because we wanted something sacred and private. We purposely drove to Titusville, Florida, so we could hide our marriage from our family until we were ready to share the news.

It wasn't rebellion. It wasn't shame. It was protection.

We wanted that moment to belong to us first. Before opinions. Before reactions. Before expectations. There was something almost poetic about choosing a quiet city on the coast to seal a covenant that would change both of our lives forever.

We stood there—just us—and stepped into forever.

She looked radiant. I looked nervous. But I also looked certain. I wasn't marrying a stranger. I wasn't marrying convenience. I wasn't marrying pressure. I was marrying my best friend.

The woman who had talked to me for 12 hours and 31 minutes across state lines. The woman who trusted me enough to move her life back to Florida. The woman who believed in a version of me that wasn't fully developed yet.

When I stood there and said my vows, I meant them. I meant every word.

But here's what I've learned since then: Meaning it in the moment is not the same as maintaining it in the years that follow. Marriage is beautiful. Marriage is holy. But marriage is hard. It exposes your wounds. It reveals your weaknesses. It magnifies your unhealed places.

And the very love that feels like redemption can also become a mirror.

We dreamed about our first home. We dreamed about family. We dreamed about building wealth and stability and something that would last. And for a season, we did. But life is not a straight line. Love does not eliminate struggle.

And sometimes the same man who marries with hope must later wrestle with habits, mental health, identity, and pressure in ways he never anticipated. And here is the part that still humbles me: Titusville—the place where we secretly began our marriage—would later become a location for a mental health hospitalization stay. The same city that held our private covenant would later hold one of my lowest battles. The same streets that witnessed our vows would later witness my vulnerability.

Joy and crisis. Covenant and collapse. Beginning and breaking—in the same place.

Still—I will never erase August 17, 2007.

Because that day was real. That love was real. That connection was real.

That 12-hour, 31-minute, and 59-second phone call was real. And I believe with everything in me that God ordained it. Even the parts that later hurt. Even the parts that later broke. Because redemption doesn't mean everything lasts forever. Sometimes redemption means God gives you a chapter that changes you—even if it doesn't stay the way you imagined.

I married my best friend that day. And even though life would later shift in ways neither of us expected, I will always honor that covenant moment. Because that day represented hope.

And hope, even when it evolves, is still sacred.

WHAT THIS MEANS FOR YOUR LIFE

Marriage is beautiful. Marriage is holy. Marriage is also the most honest mirror you will ever stand in front of.

The same city where we secretly sealed our vows—Titusville—would later hold one of my darkest mental health hospitalizations. Joy and crisis. Covenant and collapse. Beginning and breaking—in the same place.

I share that not to discourage you but to prepare you. If you are married, about to be married, or hoping to be: **love does not eliminate struggle. It exposes it.** Marriage does not cure your wounds. It reveals them. And the person you marry will see parts of you that you didn't even know existed.

That is not a flaw in marriage; that is the design of marriage. God uses covenant to surface the things He wants to heal.

If your marriage is struggling, ask yourself this: "Is the problem between us—or is it something within me that marriage is exposing?" Often the answer is both. And both require attention.

APPLY THIS

- If married: Identify one unhealed wound in your life that your marriage has revealed. Bring it to God—and if possible, to a counselor—before it becomes your spouse's burden.
- If single: Resist the belief that marriage will fix your loneliness, your identity, or your worth. Those things must be settled before the vows, not after.

- Pray for your marriage—or your future one—not just for happiness, but for honesty.

IF YOU'RE IN A GROUP

- Thoris says marriage is "the most honest mirror you will ever stand in front of." What has marriage (or a close relationship) revealed about you that you didn't expect?
- How do you maintain covenant when crisis enters your home?
- What is the difference between romance and covenant?

Prayer: Father God, thank you for the gift of covenant. Where marriage has become a mirror, give me the courage to face what it reveals. Heal the wounds I brought into the relationship before they become my partner's burden. Make our love honest, our vows holy, and our home a place where Your presence dwells. In Jesus's name. Amen.

"Some covenants change your life forever—even if they don't look the way you thought they would."

CHAPTER 10

THE RESPONSIBILITY WE DIDN'T PLAN FOR

Written by Thoris Lamar Burt

"Religion that God our Father accepts as pure and faultless is this: to look after orphans and widows in their distress . . . "

JAMES 1:27 (NIV)

Newlywed life is supposed to be light.

It's supposed to be date nights. Weekend trips. Late mornings. Dream-building. Two people learning each other slowly . . . without pressure.

That's what I thought the first few years of our marriage would look like.

We had plans.

We were going to travel. We were going to enjoy being young. We were going to build financially. We were going to start our family when we were ready.

I had a blueprint in my mind of how our first years would unfold, but God had other plans. Not long after we were newlyweds, everything shifted. My wife's nieces needed a home. Not temporarily. Not casually. They needed stability.

They were toddlers. Two little girls. Still small enough to need constant supervision. Still young enough to need daycare. Still at the age where bedtime routines and safety meant everything.

And suddenly the question became: Would we take them in?

I remember feeling a tightening in my chest the first time the conversation became real. I was the only one working. We were newly married. We were barely settled. And I was terrified. Terrified of daycare costs. Terrified of groceries doubling. Terrified of rent, utilities, diapers, medical bills. Terrified that I wouldn't be able to provide.

As the head of my household, provision wasn't optional; it was identity. And what hurt even deeper was this: Their grandmother was willing to take one of the girls—but not both.

I could not understand that. How do you separate sisters? How do you choose one child and not the other? That part disturbed me. And what further disturbed me was this: My wife had eleven siblings. Eleven. And yet we were the first ones called when something needed to be resolved. Why us? Why the newlyweds? Why the only couple still trying to find their footing?

I remember the argument like it was yesterday. I wasn't yelling out of cruelty. I was speaking from fear. I told my wife I didn't understand why it had to be us. I told her I didn't understand why none of the other siblings were stepping up. I told her I was concerned about finances. I told her I was trying to protect our future.

I *was* trying to protect us.

But then she said something that hit me like a punch to the chest. She said, "This is something I have to do. And I will do it with or without you."

With or without you.

Those words pierced something deep. After all the vows. After all the plans. After the dreams we spoke across that twelve-hour phone call years before. She was willing to risk our marriage over this.

And in that moment, I didn't feel noble. I didn't feel spiritual. I felt replaced.

I left the house upset. Not angry in a loud way. Angry in a wounded way. I got in my car and just sat there. Because this wasn't about money anymore. It was about leadership. It was about pride. It was about what kind of man I was going to be.

I prayed. Not a polished prayer. Not a church prayer. A desperate one. "God, what am I supposed to do? I don't know how to carry this. I don't know how to afford this. I don't know how to lead this."

And in that stillness—in the quiet of that parked car—something shifted. It wasn't dramatic. It wasn't thunder. It was peace. A calmness that did not make sense based on the math, and I knew it was only God.

He whispered to me: "If you trust Me with this responsibility, I will be there with you every step of the way. Cast your worries onto Me."

The fear didn't vanish, but the resistance did. And that's the difference. I went back inside the house. I looked at my wife and told her, "God gave me the green light. We're moving forward."

That moment changed us. It was no longer about what we wanted; it was about who we were becoming. The girls moved in. And our honeymoon phase ended overnight.

Daycare schedules replaced spontaneous weekends. Budget spreadsheets replaced travel planning. Discipline conversations replaced romantic dinners.

We were no longer just husband and wife. We were guardians. We were responsible for shaping two lives that had already experienced instability.

And I would be lying if I said I didn't wrestle internally. There were nights I stared at the ceiling, wondering how I would stretch 1 paycheck across 4 people. There were moments I felt resentment—not toward the girls—but toward the siblings who stayed silent.

But here's what happened next. A few weeks after we made the decision, I was blessed with a promotion at work. Not months later. Weeks. And the financial increase came right when we needed it most.

It was as if heaven was saying, "You obeyed. Now watch Me move."

Then something else happened. My wife's former employer—the wealthy family she worked for as a nanny in Connecticut—reached out with unsolicited support. They sent help. Not because we asked. Not because we demanded. But because God moved on their hearts.

Provision showed up from places we didn't even expect. Clothes. Financial support. Encouragement.

It humbled me. Because I had sat in that car afraid of lack, and God responded with overflow.

That season shaped me more than I understood at the time. It taught me that leadership is not about control—it's about surrender. It taught me that being the head of your household doesn't mean you always know the plan. It means you seek God when you don't. It taught me that fatherhood sometimes finds you before you think you're ready.

And here's the part that still brings emotion to my voice: Those little girls became part of our family story. They weren't temporary. They were divine assignments.

And even though our marriage would later face storms, I will never regret the day we said yes. Because that yes grew me up. It broke selfishness. It stretched my faith. It exposed my fear. And it showed me what happens when obedience collides with provision.

We had a blueprint. God had a calling. And that turning point—the argument, the prayer, the surrender—became one of the most defining moments of our marriage. Not because it was easy. But because it forced us to choose who we were going to be.

WHAT THIS MEANS FOR YOUR LIFE

When my wife said, "I will do it with or without you," I didn't feel noble; I felt replaced. But that sentence forced me to make a decision about who I was going to be: a man who protects comfort, or a man who protects children.

If God has placed an unexpected responsibility in your lap—a relative's child, an aging parent, a community need that nobody else is addressing—I want you to know two things: Your fear is valid, and your obedience is still required.

Fear and obedience are not opposites. You can be terrified and still say yes. In fact, the most sacred acts of obedience in Scripture were accompanied by fear. Abraham. Moses. Mary. Every one of them was afraid. Every one of them obeyed anyway.

And here is the part that still stuns me: Weeks after we said yes, I received a promotion. My wife's former employer sent unsolicited support. Provision showed up from places we didn't expect. That is what happens when obedience collides with God's assignment. He doesn't always remove the fear, but He always covers the faith.

APPLY THIS

- What unexpected responsibility has God placed in your life that you've been resisting?
- If fear is the reason you haven't said yes, name the specific fear. Is it financial? Relational? Reputational? Name it and bring it to God.

- Look for the provision. If you've already said yes to something hard, pause and look around. Where has God already begun to provide? Write it down before you forget.

IF YOU'RE IN A GROUP

- Have you ever been asked to take on a responsibility you didn't plan for? How did you respond?
- Thoris says, "Fear and obedience are not opposites." How does that change the way you approach scary decisions?
- What is the difference between protecting your comfort and protecting your future?

Prayer: Father God, when You place unexpected responsibility in my hands, give me the courage to say yes before I feel ready. Replace my fear with faith. Replace my hesitation with obedience. Provide what I need to carry what You've assigned and remind me that You don't always remove the fear—but You always cover the faith. In Jesus's name. Amen.

"Fear and obedience are not opposites. You can be terrified and still say yes—and when you do, God always covers the faith."

CHAPTER 11

A MOTHER'S RELEASE

Written by Carolyn Virginia Burt

"As a mother comforts her child, so will I comfort you; and you will be comforted."

ISAIAH 66:13 (NIV)

When Thoris got married, I smiled on the outside—but inside, I was grieving.

Not because I didn't love his wife. Not because I didn't want him to be happy. But because I felt like I had just handed over the one person who had walked beside me through everything.

Thoris was not just my son. He was my helper. My companion. My steady one.

He did everything for his mother.

When I bought my 2001 Acura MDX SUV, he paid the down payment without hesitation. He paid my monthly car note for a while.

He made sure my oil was changed. If something in my house needed fixing, he showed up. If I had a doctor's appointment, he made sure I got there. He carried more than responsibility—he carried me in ways he didn't even realize.

So, when he got married, I knew the order of things. I raised him to leave and cleave. I raised him to be a provider. I raised him to protect his household.

But I was not prepared for how quiet my life would feel after.

Phone calls became shorter. Decisions were no longer run through me. The rhythm we had built shifted overnight. I told myself, "Carolyn, this is how it's supposed to be."

But the heart doesn't always obey logic.

There were moments I sat in my house and felt replaced. I didn't say it out loud; I prayed about it instead. I asked God to remove any bitterness from me. I asked Him to help me celebrate my son without resenting the change.

It was a hard pill to swallow.

WHAT THIS MEANS FOR YOUR LIFE

To every mother reading this: Releasing your child to their own life is not betrayal. It is the final assignment of good parenting.

But nobody prepares you for how quiet the house gets. Nobody tells you that the phone calls will become shorter. Nobody warns you that decisions will be made without your input. Nobody explains that the child you carried will build a life you were not consulted on—and that this is exactly how it's supposed to be.

Release is not loss. Release is trust. You are trusting that what you planted in them will hold. And if it doesn't hold perfectly, you are trusting God to cover the gaps.

Your role did not end; it evolved. You are no longer the architect of their daily life. You are the prayer covering over their entire life. That is not a demotion; that is a promotion.

APPLY THIS

- If you are struggling to release an adult child, identify one specific area where you are still trying to control or be consulted. Ask God to help you release it.
- Replace control with prayer. For every urge to call and "check," pray instead. Let God be the one who checks on them.
- Tell your child you're proud of them. Say it out loud. This week.

IF YOU'RE IN A GROUP

- Carolyn says she "felt replaced" when Thoris got married. Is that a common feeling among parents? How do you navigate it?
- What does it look like to release a child without losing connection?
- How do you balance being available with respecting their independence?

Prayer: Father God, thank you for trusting me to raise my children, and now thank you for trusting me to release them. Where I have tried to control, teach me to pray. Where I have grieved the change, remind me that release is not loss—it is faith. Cover my children where my hands no longer reach and let my prayers be the canopy beneath which they walk. In Jesus's name. Amen.

"A mother may release her son to marriage—but she never releases him from prayer."

CHAPTER 12

WHEN I FOUND OUT TOO LATE

Written by Carolyn Virginia Burt

"Surely you desire truth in the inner parts; you teach me wisdom in the inmost place."

PSALM 51:6 (NIV)

When I learned from my daughter Tracy that Thoris had moved his new wife and her nieces into my home, I was in total shock.

It was not that I did not want him married. It was not that I did not love children in my house. It was that I did not know.

There is a particular sting that comes when you find out something important through someone else; it feels like you were the last to be told. And when truth arrives late, trust feels bruised.

When I found out that the girls had taken over my master bedroom, I was very upset. That room meant something to me. It was not just square footage. It represented years of sacrifice. It represented the nights I stayed up praying. It represented ownership—something I had worked hard to maintain as a single mother.

Looking back now, I can admit something hard: I was being selfish.

At that time, I had recently relocated back to Huntsville, Alabama, for a promotion. I was proud of that promotion. I had labored for years. I had climbed professional hills while raising children alone. Moving back to Huntsville was both a promotion and a full-circle moment.

But even though I had relocated, part of my heart still lived in that house in Orlando. The master bedroom was empty physically, but emotionally, it was not.

Terrell was living in my home with Thoris at the time. Later, Terrell told me that he was not trying to act grown, but he felt like he was going to have to move out because Thoris now had a wife and family there.

That worried me.

As a mother, I did not want one son who was adjusting to marriage while the other felt displaced. I felt responsible for making sure neither one of them felt unstable.

So, I stepped in.

I helped Terrell secure an apartment. I paid his rent. I made sure he had what he needed.

That is what mothers do. We stretch ourselves financially and emotionally to keep our children steady.

Thoris paid me rent faithfully. At the age of thirty, he was a responsible young man. That responsibility was the very reason I trusted him to oversee my home while I moved back to Huntsville.

He had proven himself dependable, but communication was missing. And sometimes, the pain is not about the action—it is about not being included in the conversation.

I wish he had called me first. I wish I had heard it from him. I wish I had been prepared.

Instead, I found out too late.

God has a way of allowing time to mature your perspective.

The truth is it was an empty room. The truth is those girls needed stability. The truth is my son was trying to lead his household.

And perhaps my hurt was not about a bedroom at all. Perhaps it was about transition. Motherhood changes when your children marry. You are no longer consulted on every decision. You are no longer the first voice in their daily lives. You have to trust what you poured into them.

That is not easy.

But God remained faithful through it all. He allowed me to pay my mortgage in Orlando. He allowed me to pay my apartment rent in Huntsville. He allowed me to help Terrell with his rent as well.

That was not my strength alone; that was provision. God has taken care of my children and me for a long time. Even when my feelings were strong. Even when pride tried to rise. Even when communication fell short. He provided. He covered. He corrected my heart.

Psalm 51:6 says that God desires truth in the inner parts. That means being honest with yourself. The honest truth is this: I felt left out. I felt hurt. I felt replaced.

But I was also blessed. Blessed that my sons were responsible men. Blessed that my home was still a place of refuge. Blessed that God provided for all of us. Blessed that even when I found out too late, God was not late in teaching me wisdom.

He is an awesome God. And I will never stop serving Him.

WHAT THIS MEANS FOR YOUR LIFE

When truth arrives late, the pain is not about the information. It's about the exclusion. "Why didn't you tell me?" is really asking, "Do I still matter to you?"

If you are on either side of this—the one who found out late, or the one who didn't communicate—here is the principle: **Communication is not just about transferring information. Communication is about honoring relationship.** When you make a major decision without including someone who loves you, even if the decision is good, the exclusion wounds them.

And to the person who found out late, the honest truth is often this—the decision that was made without you was probably not about disrespecting you. It was about someone navigating their own pressure in real time and not having the bandwidth to include everyone. That doesn't make it right, but understanding it might help you forgive it.

APPLY THIS

- Is there something you need to communicate to a family member that you've been avoiding? Do it this week.
- Is there something you found out late that you're still carrying resentment about? Write down what hurt more—the action or the exclusion. Then bring that specific hurt to God.
- Make a practice of over-communicating with the people you love. It is always better to say too much than to leave someone feeling excluded.

IF YOU'RE IN A GROUP

- Have you ever found out something important about a family member's life after the fact? How did it make you feel?
- Carolyn admits, "I was being selfish." How hard is it to distinguish between legitimate hurt and selfishness in family conflicts?
- What role does pride play in communication breakdowns within families?

Prayer: Father God, search my heart and remove pride where it lingers. Teach me to communicate with grace and receive change with maturity. Thank you for always providing for my children and me. Continue teaching me wisdom in the inmost place. In Jesus's name. Amen.

"When truth arrives late,

it tests trust—but God

can still restore both."

PART IV

BREAKING: WHEN THE MIND TURNS (2018-2021)

Core Teaching: Mental illness is not weakness—it is illness. And even illness cannot separate you from God's purpose.

CHAPTER 13

APRIL 29, 2018–THE FIRST TIME I LOST CONTROL

Written by Thoris Lamar Burt

"I am overwhelmed with troubles and my life draws near to death. I am counted among those who go down to the pit; I am like one without strength."

PSALM 88:3-4 (NIV)

Nothing dramatic triggered it. No car accident. No public breakdown.

Just heat.

Not the kind you sweat through. Not a fever. This felt internal. Trapped. Like my skin was holding fire underneath it.

I kept taking cold showers. Cold baths. Back-to-back. Over and over. I couldn't regulate my body. I couldn't regulate my thoughts. I didn't know the word for it then, but I was experiencing tactile hallucinations—my skin felt like it was burning from the inside out.

Sleep wouldn't come.

My body was exhausted, but my mind would not shut down. That night marked what I now understand as the pattern of my episodes: insomnia first. Then distortion. Then escalation.

Even normal sounds became unbearable. A lawnmower outside didn't sound distant—it sounded like it was inside my bedroom, roaring through my skull like a jet engine. Everything was amplified. Everything felt urgent. My nervous system felt like exposed wiring.

There's a certain kind of fear that only shows up when your own mind turns against you—not fear of danger, but fear of not knowing what's real anymore.

My wife was in bed with me at some point. I don't remember what we said. I don't remember if she was afraid. I just remember that I wasn't alone—and still, I felt completely isolated inside my own head.

Then there was a knock.

Loud.

Authoritative.

Someone said it was the police.

When I looked outside, I saw flashing lights. Six patrol cars. EMT trucks. A firetruck. It didn't make sense. It felt cinematic. Exaggerated. Like I had stepped into a ThunderCats episode instead of my own life.

I didn't have clothes on. I had taken them off, trying to cool down.

When I opened the door, six officers rushed in.

Everything escalated instantly.

They pushed me to the floor. I kept asking what I had done wrong. I kept telling them they were hurting me. I wasn't resisting; I was confused. No one explained anything. No one slowed it down.

I don't know when Crisis Intervention Training became standard in Orlando, but that night, that is not who showed up.

Force showed up.

And force inside confusion feels like confirmation that you are dangerous.

In my hallucinating state, I thought I was a ThunderCat. I flipped off the bed and landed in a stance like Lion-O himself.

It sounds almost absurd now, but it wasn't then. My brain was searching for identity, for strength, for a narrative that made sense. It grabbed onto childhood mythology because reality was slipping.

Before I knew it, I was handcuffed tightly and dragged down my stairs.

Half-naked.

Confused.

Terrified.

I remember hitting the walls. I remember not being able to brace myself. I remember humiliation attaching itself to trauma.

When I got outside, everything slowed down.

I saw my mama.

She was crying hysterically, begging them not to hurt her baby.

That image has never left me.

Later, I would learn that my wife and a close family friend, who was a nurse, had called 911 because I was having a medical emergency—not because I was violent, not because I had committed a crime.

That distinction matters.

I don't remember the ride clearly. Trauma doesn't record clean footage. But I remember fear. I remember losing control of my narrative. I remember realizing my life had become an emergency, and I did not understand why.

At Florida Hospital East, the paranoia intensified. I believed I had been drugged. I believed people were against me.

Psychosis fills in blanks with threat.

They ran tests. I remember an invasive drug screening that remains one of the most physically painful and humiliating moments of my life. I remember hearing someone mention opioids in my system—real or hallucinated, I still don't know.

That uncertainty haunts me. Because when your mind betrays you, even evidence feels unstable.

I remember being hospitalized.

Medication was introduced—names I didn't yet understand. Side effects I couldn't anticipate. I remember sitting in group therapy rooms, surrounded by strangers whose pain looked different but felt familiar.

Time felt suspended.

I don't remember how long I stayed. I only remember the shift.

April 29, 2018, was the first documented episode. The first time my private mental struggle became a public crisis. The first time I felt my autonomy stripped away.

And that feeling of loss—loss of control—followed me. Into my marriage. Into my career. Into every interview room where I tried to prove I was still competent. Into every conversation where I tried to prove I was still trustworthy.

After that night, I was no longer just ambitious or driven or stressed.

I was a patient.

Since then, there have been more episodes. More hospitalizations. Some memories are clear; others fragmented. During later stays, I remember being handled roughly—body-slammed, restrained, pushed. Some bruises were real. Some were tactile hallucinations.

In 2025, a doctor from my church gently told me that entire conversations I remembered never actually happened.

That revelation unsettled me deeply.

If I cannot trust my memory, what can I trust?

Every time I feel insomnia creeping in now, my paranoia rises. Admission doesn't feel like safety—it feels like surrender. It feels like losing dignity before I can explain myself.

But here is what I know now that I didn't know then: April 29, 2018, was not weakness.

It was illness.

It was the first time my brain crossed a line that required medical intervention.

And even in that chaos—even in the confusion, the force, the humiliation—God did not leave me.

He whispered later what I couldn't hear then: "My grace is sufficient. My power works in your weakness."

That night felt like the loss of control. But it was also the beginning of understanding. Nothing after April 29, 2018, can be understood without it.

WHAT THIS MEANS FOR YOUR LIFE

There is a moment in the life of every person who lives with mental illness when the diagnosis stops being abstract and becomes an address. April 29, 2018, was my change of address.

I want to teach you something the church has been reluctant to say clearly: **Mental illness is not a character flaw. It is not a faith failure.**

It is not a demon that can be prayed away with enough volume. It is illness. And illness requires treatment.

Here is what I wish I had known before April 29, 2018—and what I want you to know right now:

Insomnia is often the first warning. Before the hallucinations, before the psychosis, before the paranoia—there was sleeplessness. When someone you love stops sleeping, do not dismiss it. That is the canary in the coal mine. Pay attention.

A mental health crisis is a medical emergency, not a behavioral problem. When 911 is called for a mental health episode, it should be treated with the same urgency and compassion as a heart attack. The person is not being difficult. Their brain is malfunctioning. The fact that you can't see it on an X-ray does not make it less real.

What to do if someone you love is in crisis: Call 988 (the Suicide and Crisis Lifeline). If you call 911, tell the dispatcher explicitly that it is a mental health crisis and request CIT-trained officers if available. Stay calm. Speak softly. Do not argue with hallucinations or delusions. Reduce stimulation—lower lights, turn off loud sounds. Do not take their behavior personally.

The person in crisis did not choose this. And the way you respond in that first hour may shape how they view help for the rest of their life.

APPLY THIS

- Save the number 988 in your phone right now. You may never need it. But if you do, you won't have time to search for it.

- Learn whether your local police department has CIT-trained officers or a Community Response Team. If they do, learn how to request them specifically.
- If you live with a mental health condition, identify your early warning signs. Write them down. Share them with one trusted person.

IF YOU'RE IN A GROUP

- How does your church currently respond when a member experiences a mental health crisis? How should it respond?
- Thoris describes the difference between being treated as a patient versus being treated as a problem. Have you witnessed that difference?
- What would change in your family if mental illness were treated the same as any other medical condition?

Prayer: Father God, thank you for being present in the moments my mind could not understand reality. Thank you for sending help when I could not call for it myself. For every person living with mental illness, I pray now—cover them, advocate for them, send them clinicians and officers and family members who treat them like patients, not problems. Remind them that even when their mind betrays them, You never will. In Jesus's name. Amen.

> *What I describe in this chapter is my own experience, not a diagnosis or a treatment plan. If any of it sounds like your life, please talk to a mental-health professional—and if you are in danger right now, call or text 988. —T.*

"Nothing prepares you for the moment when your life becomes an emergency and you don't understand why—only that it is happening to you."

CHAPTER 14

A MOTHER'S FIGHT

Written by Carolyn Virginia Burt

"The Lord will fight for you; you need only to be still."

EXODUS 14:14 (NIV)

It didn't matter that he was grown. It didn't matter that he was married. In that moment, I didn't see a husband or a man—I saw the little boy I carried.

The shock overwhelmed me. I remember passing out. By the time I regained consciousness, they had placed him in an ambulance and were about to transport him to the mental health facility near UCF.

No mother is prepared for that sight.

The next day, I went to visit him. I walked into that facility praying under my breath. When I stepped into his room, he looked at me—but he did not know who I was.

That pain is indescribable.

I hugged him anyway. I held him tightly. Thoris laid his head on my shoulder just like he had done when he was a child. For a moment, it didn't matter that he didn't recognize me. My body recognized him. My spirit recognized him.

One of the nurses asked, "Are you his mom?"

I said, "Yes."

She replied, "I can tell by the way you are hugging him."

That statement stayed with me. A mother's embrace does not require permission. It does not require memory. It does not require recognition.

He stayed there for about two weeks. I visited him almost every day. I prayed in my car before walking inside. I prayed over his bed. I prayed over his mind. I reminded God of His promises. I told the Lord, "You gave him to me. You cannot let the enemy take him like this."

After he was released, his father and I asked for a copy of his bloodwork. Weeks passed before we received it.

When I finally saw the report, my eyes immediately went to one word: opioids.

My heart dropped.

I asked his wife, "Is Thoris on drugs?"

She replied, "I don't know who's trying to kill him."

I said, "Who said anything about killing somebody?"

But then I asked, "Who is trying to kill him?" There was no answer.

My son has never been on drugs. He has never smoked. He does not drink alcohol. The presence of opioids in his system was never fully explained. But I know this: That was the first time—and the last time.

I went home that night and fell on my knees.

I realized something in that season. When Thoris got married, I thought I was losing my best friend. But in that hospital room, I realized I could have lost my son entirely.

God had to teach me the difference between release and loss. Release is painful—but it is healthy. Loss is devastating—but it is not permanent when God intervenes.

I had to learn how to let my son build his own family while still covering him in prayer. I had to learn that I could no longer hold the first place in his life—but I would always be his mother.

Marriage changed our relationship. Mental illness tested our faith. But neither one removed me from his life.

There is a fight that only a mother knows how to fight. It is fought on her knees. It is fought in the midnight hours. It is fought with tears and Scripture.

I may have felt like I gave my son away when he got married.

But when I saw him confused, vulnerable, and unaware of who I was, I understood something deeper. He was never mine to possess. He was entrusted to me. And even when I had to release him to a wife … even when I had to release him to doctors … even when I had to release him to an ambulance... I never released him from prayer.

God saved my child. And that is why HE kept him.

WHAT THIS MEANS FOR YOUR LIFE

To every parent with a child who struggles with mental illness: You are not powerless. But you are not the cure, either. Your child needs your prayer, your presence, and your willingness to let professionals do what love alone cannot.

The hardest thing I've ever seen my mama do was stand outside a facility and trust strangers with her baby, but she did it. Because she understood that love sometimes means stepping back so treatment can step in.

What parents of adult children with mental illness need to hear:

You did not cause this. You cannot control this. But you can support the process.

Educate yourself on their diagnosis. Attend family therapy if offered. Ask their treatment team how you can help—not how you can take over. Love them loudly but let go gently.

And pray. Pray in your car. Pray in the parking lot. Pray over their bed. Pray when they don't recognize you. Pray especially then.

APPLY THIS

- If you are a parent of someone with mental illness, identify one way you've been trying to control the situation instead of supporting the process. Release it to God.
- Learn one new thing about your loved one's diagnosis this week. Knowledge replaces fear.
- Take care of yourself. Caregiver burnout is real. You cannot pour from an empty cup.

IF YOU'RE IN A GROUP

- Carolyn says, "A mother's embrace does not require permission." What does that mean to you?
- How do you balance being present for a loved one in crisis without losing yourself in the process?
- What is the hardest part of watching someone you love struggle with something you can't fix?

Prayer: Father God, You are the parent of every child who suffers, and You feel every weight a mother carries. For every parent watching their child battle mental illness, give them strength they did not know they had. Equip them to advocate, to pray, to step back when treatment must step in, and to keep loving when love is all they have left to offer. Fight for them, Lord. In Jesus's name. Amen.

"A mother's embrace does

not require permission.

And a mother's prayers

do not require sleep."

CHAPTER 15

BUT GOD—A LIVING BENEFITS MIRACLE

Written by Thoris Lamar Burt

"Now to him who is able to do immeasurably more than all we ask or imagine, according to his power that is at work within us."

EPHESIANS 3:20 (NIV)

I'm a firm believer that things don't happen to us—they happen for us. And sometimes, God will let something shake you just enough to redirect you . . . and bless you in a way you never saw coming.

Sometimes the shake-up feels like loss. Sometimes it feels like fear. Sometimes it feels like embarrassment or pain. But if you stay still long enough to listen, you'll realize that what felt like destruction was actually divine interruption.

February 27, 2021, was one of those days. It started like any other day, and that's what makes it so sobering. Life-changing days rarely announce themselves.

I took one of my nieces on a college tour in Miami. Everything was normal—good energy, good weather, and good vegan food from a popular spot we decided to try. I finished eating, stood up to throw away my trash... and suddenly felt lightheaded. A wave hit me so hard, I had to sit back down.

It wasn't dramatic at first. Just a shift. A quiet warning my body tried to give me. I assumed it was because I had donated blood the night before and I hadn't properly refueled. Plus, I had driven us all the way to Miami on an empty stomach because I'd been so focused on getting my niece there on time.

That's how we are sometimes—so busy showing up for others that we ignore the signals in our own bodies.

After a moment, I stood up again. I thought I was fine. But a few minutes later, while taking a picture with the restaurant owner, it happened again. The dizziness—but stronger. This time, everything went black.

There is something humbling about blacking out. One second you are standing, thinking you're in control. The next second, you're nothing but weight in freefall.

When I opened my eyes, I was on the ground. Flat on my back. My wife was hovering over me, trying to revive me. I had collapsed and hit my chest, chin, and face on the back of the food truck. My wife said I had been out for forty seconds.

Forty seconds may not sound like long. But when someone you love is unconscious on concrete, it feels like eternity.

I didn't want to go to the hospital in Miami. I felt in my spirit that if I went to the ER there, they were going to keep me. So, I told everyone, "Don't call 911. I'll get checked out when I'm back in Orlando."

Looking back, I realize how stubborn that sounds. But fear does that. Fear makes you negotiate with danger.

We drove to my Auntie Shirley's house near Dolphin Stadium. She pleaded with me to go to the ER—but all I wanted was to lie down for an hour. After resting, my wife drove us back to Orlando, and the moment we arrived, I went straight to AdventHealth East.

They ran an EKG. It was abnormal. They admitted me immediately—just like I knew they would. Sometimes your spirit knows before your mind catches up. During their tests, they discovered I had 40% blockage in my heart. That meant I had suffered a mild heart attack.

The words "heart attack" do something to you. They make you replay your life in fast-forward. They make you think about unfinished conversations, unpaid debts, broken relationships, and the people who would have to live without you.

The cardiologist told me, "If you weren't vegan, your blockage would've been much higher. You would've needed a stent." But God…

I didn't need surgery. I didn't need anything except monitoring, clean eating, and more exercise.

That *But God* carried weight.

Because it could have been worse. It should have been worse. By statistics alone, it often is worse.

What I didn't know was that God wasn't done turning this situation around for my good. Because of that heart condition—documented and confirmed—I qualified for Living Benefits under my term life insurance policy. And what came next was nothing short of a miracle: a six-figure payout. Tax-free. No repayment. No strings attached.

Let that sink in.

A collapse in a parking lot. A diagnosis that shook me. And then provision I didn't see coming.

I'd paid around $3,000 total into that policy since I'd purchased it in 2016 . . . and it yielded a tax-free, six-figure return that changed my entire financial landscape. This was the provision that allowed me to keep my home during my divorce and I am forever grateful.

That payout wasn't just money. It was breathing room. It was relief. It was proof that preparation meets providence. Some people don't believe in life insurance until it's too late. I'm here to tell you: Don't sleep on it. Life insurance isn't just about death—it's about living, protecting, and accessing blessings in unexpected seasons. It's about wisdom before crisis. It's about stewardship before storms. It's about trusting God enough to prepare while everything looks stable.

This wasn't luck. This wasn't coincidence. This was God doing what Ephesians 3:20 promised—immeasurably more than I could ask or imagine.

Not just saving my life. Not just preventing surgery. But flipping a medical scare into financial restoration.

A collapse that could've killed me... turned into a financial blessing that restored me. *But God.*

And the miracle wasn't just the money. The miracle was the message.

Slow down. Take care of your body. Prepare for the unexpected. Trust Me with the outcome.

Sometimes the blessing is not in avoiding the fall. Sometimes the blessing is in what God builds after you hit the ground.

WHAT THIS MEANS FOR YOUR LIFE

This chapter is about stewardship before crisis.

I paid approximately $3,000 into a life insurance policy and received a six-figure tax-free payout through Living Benefits when I was diagnosed with a heart condition. That math doesn't make sense in the natural, but it makes perfect sense in the kingdom.

Here is what I want every reader to do after reading this chapter:

If you do not have life insurance, get it. This week. Not next month. Not when you "can afford it." Now.

If you already have life insurance, call your provider and ask this question: "Does my policy include a Living Benefits or Accelerated Death Benefit rider?" If it does, understand what qualifies you to access it. If it doesn't, ask what it would cost to add one.

Life insurance is not just about death. It is about living. It is about accessing resources during critical illness, chronic conditions, or terminal diagnoses—while you are still alive.

Preparation is an act of faith. You are not preparing because you expect the worst. You are preparing because you trust God to use every tool you give Him.

APPLY THIS

- If you don't have life insurance, research a term life policy this week. Many affordable options exist. Start there.
- If you have life insurance, call your provider and ask about Living Benefits. Know what you have before you need it.
- Create or update your emergency file. Life insurance info, bank accounts, passwords, medical records. If something happens to you tomorrow, would your family know where to find everything?
- Share this chapter with someone who doesn't have life insurance. This information could change a family's future.

IF YOU'RE IN A GROUP

- Did you know that life insurance can pay out while you're still alive? How does that change your perspective on it?
- Thoris says, "Preparation is an act of faith." How does that challenge the idea that preparation shows a lack of trust in God?
- What practical steps can you take this week to be better prepared for the unexpected?

Prayer: Father God, thank you for the wisdom of preparation. Thank you for resources I didn't know I would need until I needed them.

Teach me to be a good steward of every tool You've placed in my hands—insurance, savings, faith, and family. Where I have neglected preparation, give me the discipline to begin today, and let my preparedness become a testimony of Your provision. In Jesus's name. Amen.

"When God steps in, even the things meant to break you become the blessings that build you."

PART V

SHATTERING: THE VALLEY OF THE SHADOW (2022-2024)

Core Teaching: The darkest valley is where God does His most sacred work.

CHAPTER 16

LOVE AFTER LOSS: MY DIVORCE STORY

Written by Thoris Lamar Burt

"The Lord is nigh unto them that are of a broken heart; and saveth such as be of a contrite spirit."

PSALM 34:18

I married my best friend on August 17, 2007. We were young, hopeful, and ready to build a life together. What I didn't expect was that our story would also include raising her nieces—2 beautiful little girls, only 2 and 4 years old.

I couldn't see how we were going to manage it. But my wife—she was determined. Fierce. Protective. She refused to let those girls end up in the foster system.

I still hear her words: "If I have to raise them without you, I will."

And that caused a rift early in our marriage. Not because we didn't love each other—but because the responsibility was heavy, unexpected, and real.

Still, we loved those girls. We created memories. We built a life that, for a time, felt steady and beautiful.

And there was a blessing in that season I will never forget. On January 29, 2013, we closed on our first home—a house we didn't just buy, but built from the ground up, exactly the way we had envisioned it. We picked the lot. We watched the frame rise out of Florida dirt and become walls, become rooms, become ours. Standing in that finished house with the keys in my hand, I felt like God had taken the picture we carried in our hearts and made it real. It was one of the most impactful moments of our marriage—proof that two people, hoping together, could build something that lasts.

But love doesn't erase wounds—especially the ones we create ourselves.

My impulsive behavior—the very thing tied to my schizoaffective disorder (bipolar type)—pulled me into infidelity. My wife gave me chance after chance after chance to stop cheating on her whether it was physical and/or emotional... but when a woman is fed up, you feel it in her silence long before she says the words.

And I couldn't blame her. Trust, once broken, is hard to rebuild, and I waited too long to fight for what mattered.

But what broke me, what left a scar deeper than the divorce itself, was learning that fear also played a role.

The fear that I wasn't taking my medication. The fear that one day I might harm myself... or harm our family... because of misunderstandings about mental illness.

It wasn't until after the marriage was over that a Black male psychiatrist—Maurice Foster—told me something that changed everything: "You can be fully compliant with your medication and still experience mental episodes. The goal isn't perfection—it's awareness, support, and grace."

But Maurice Foster didn't stop at education. He moved into action. He ordered a test I'd never heard of before—a GeneSight test. It's a pharmacogenomic test that analyzes your DNA from a simple cheek swab and tells the doctor which mental health medications are most likely to work with your specific genetic makeup, which ones may cause side effects, and which ones your body may not metabolize well at all.

Think about that for a moment. For decades, psychiatry has often been trial and error. A doctor prescribes a medication, you take it for weeks or months, and if it doesn't work or the side effects become unbearable, you switch to another one. Then another. Then another. All while you're trying to live your life, hold down a job, parent your children, and stay sane in the middle of a chemical experiment being conducted on your own brain.

GeneSight changed that. Instead of guessing, my psychiatrist could now look at my actual DNA and say, "These medications align with your genetic profile. These don't. Let's start with what your body is already designed to process well."

That kit arrived at my house in a plain FedEx envelope. I swabbed the inside of my cheeks, sealed it up, and mailed it back. A few weeks later, my psychiatrist had a report that helped him make medication decisions based on science instead of guesswork.

I wish we had known that truth sooner—both about compliance and about the science available to us. I wish we all understood that schizoaffective disorder isn't linear, predictable, or clean. But we learned it the hard way.

When I returned from Huntsville after Thanksgiving in 2022, I walked into a truth I wasn't ready to face: It was over.

On December 19, 2022, the divorce became official.

I had loved deeply, and now I had to grieve deeply. But even in that valley, God never abandoned me.

Through every tear, He whispered, "I am still here."

Through every night I replayed conversations, mistakes, and memories, He reminded me, "You are still My child."

The heartbreak didn't destroy me—it redirected me. It stripped away what was fragile, so God could rebuild what was true. It taught me that losing love doesn't mean losing yourself—not when God is your anchor.

Today, I'm not bitter. I'm better.

Better because I understand myself. Better because I understand mental health in a way I didn't before. Better because I now know that some endings are holy—not punishments, but protection.

Real love begins after loss—because it's in that sacred place that you rediscover who you are … and more importantly … whose you are.

WHAT THIS MEANS FOR YOUR LIFE

Here is the sentence that changed everything for me. A Black male psychiatrist—Maurice Foster—told me: "You can be fully compliant with your medication and still experience mental episodes. The goal isn't perfection—it's awareness, support, and grace."

If I could go back in time and place that sentence at the beginning of my marriage, I believe the story might have ended differently.

I share that not as blame but as education. **Mental illness is not linear.** Taking medication faithfully does not guarantee a crisis-free life. It reduces frequency and intensity, but it does not eliminate the possibility of episodes entirely.

If you love someone with bipolar disorder, depression, PTSD, or any chronic mental health condition, this truth is essential: **Compliance is not a cure. Love them through the episodes, not just between them.** And if fear of their illness is driving your decisions, seek education before you seek distance.

To the person who lost a marriage because of mental health: Your diagnosis is not your disqualification. You are not unlovable. You are navigating something that requires a partner willing to learn, grow, and stay—and that is a high standard, but it is not an impossible one.

And here is something every person taking psychiatric medication needs to know: **Mental health care should not be guesswork.** Pharmacogenomic testing—like the GeneSight test Maurice Foster ordered for me—uses a simple cheek swab to analyze your DNA and identify which medications are most likely to work with your body and which ones may cause problems. Many insurance plans, including Medicare, cover these tests when ordered by a clinician for medically appropriate reasons.

If you've been on multiple medications without finding one that works—or if you've experienced severe side effects from medications that should have helped—this test could change your treatment trajectory. Your DNA is data. Your psychiatrist should have access to it.

APPLY THIS

- If you love someone with a mental health condition, educate yourself on their specific diagnosis. Attend a NAMI Family-to-Family class or read a book recommended by their therapist.
- If you lost a relationship because of your mental health, your diagnosis is not your disqualification. Write down three qualities about yourself that have nothing to do with your illness.
- If you are married and your spouse has a mental health condition, ask them, "What do you need from me during an episode?" The answer may surprise you. Often, it's just presence.
- **Ask your psychiatrist about GeneSight or pharmacogenomic testing.** If you take psychiatric medication and your provider has never mentioned this option, bring it up at your next appointment. The test could prevent years of trial-and-error prescribing.

IF YOU'RE IN A GROUP

- How does mental health stigma specifically affect marriages and romantic relationships?
- Maurice Foster said, "The goal isn't perfection—it's awareness, support, and grace." How does that standard apply to other areas of life beyond mental health?
- What would change if churches offered mental health education for couples alongside premarital counseling?
- Did you know that genetic testing exists to help match psychiatric medications to your specific DNA? How might that science change the conversation around mental health treatment in your community?

Prayer: Father God, where love has been lost, restore identity. Where divorce has shaken foundations, rebuild them on Your truth. Heal every wound mental illness inflicted on my marriage, and teach me to love again—wisely, honestly, and fully. Remind me that my diagnosis is not my disqualification, and that even endings can be holy when You are the author. In Jesus's name. Amen.

"Real healing doesn't happen when life is perfect—it happens when God rebuilds you from what's left."

CHAPTER 17

NOVEMBER 26, 2023—I ALMOST LET GO

Written by Thoris Lamar Burt

"You, Lord, brought me up from the realm of the dead; you spared me from going down to the pit."

PSALM 30:3

Some dates don't fade; they brand themselves onto your soul. They don't soften with time. They don't blur around the edges. They stay sharp—like a scar you can still feel when the weather changes.

November 26, 2023, is one of those days for me—the day the bottom dropped out. The day the storm swallowed me whole. The day I almost slipped away.

To understand that day, you have to understand the weight that was crushing me long before I stepped into that garage.

This wasn't one bad afternoon; this was months of erosion. Quiet losses. Silent shame. Internal battles no one could see. I had lost my six-figure job in 2023 because of my mental condition—and I lost my family too. My ex-wife blocked me. My nieces blocked me. My nephews blocked me. Phone. Social media. Everything. One day I had a family—the next day, it felt like I had been erased.

There is something psychologically violent about being erased. No fight. No closure. Just silence.

The money was gone—every dollar I had burned through in just twelve months. The stability was gone. The support I once leaned on … gone. And when the paycheck disappeared, so did my safety net. No spousal income. No second stream. No cushion to land on. Just interviews—and rejection after rejection.

I made it to final rounds over and over again. "You're a top candidate … we really like you … but we went with someone else because ___."

Each email felt polite. Professional. Dismissive. Every rejection pressed the depression deeper into my bones. Depression doesn't just sit in your mind. It sinks into your muscles. It makes your body heavy. It makes hope feel irresponsible.

I had been working nonstop since the age of fourteen—my first job washing dishes at the NCO Club on Redstone Arsenal. I had never been the kind of man who asked for help. But desperation has a way of stripping your pride down to nothing. So, I went to my church—the place I had been faithfully tithing at since 1993. Over three decades of consistent, sacrificial giving. And when I finally gathered the courage to ask for financial help, I was told the church had a one-time assistance policy. One time. After more than thirty years of faithfulness. That rejection cut differently than the job rejections; those came from strangers. This came from my church family—the people I had worshipped beside, served alongside, and sown into for most of my adult life. It didn't make me lose my faith in God, but it shook my faith in the institution.

I remember telling my mama one time, many years earlier, that I couldn't afford to pay for her SUV anymore. I told her I needed help. She scolded me and told me no. From that day forward, I never asked her for help again—even when she later offered to assist with the down payment on my house, I declined. Pride and pain can look the same from the outside.

At my lowest point—my savings exhausted and my spirit worn down—I didn't want to ask my daddy for help. Not because he wouldn't help, but because I didn't want to feel like a burden.

My mind whispered a dangerous lie: "If I'm gone, my house, my car, and my bills will be paid off. At least I could leave a legacy behind." I was already well beyond the suicide non-payout clause of my life insurance policy, which made the lie feel even more convincing in that moment.

That's how distorted depression can be—it dresses death up like generosity.

Attempt 1: I walked to the street and thought about running out in front of a car, hoping it would all be over instantly—but then I thought about how it could traumatize the driver, how it could ruin their life financially or emotionally. I didn't want anyone else to suffer the way I was suffering. Even in my despair, empathy stopped me.

Attempt 2: I walked to the bridge near my mama's house and thought about jumping in front of an eighteen-wheeler. But again, I thought about the impact—literally and figuratively—on innocent people. I didn't want my pain to become someone else's lifelong burden. Pain was loud. Conscience was louder.

Attempt 3: I filled up the bathtub in my master bathroom after finding a flat iron my ex-wife left behind. It got so hot, it felt like fire. I got into the tub fully clothed... but then I thought about my family finding me like that. I couldn't put them through that trauma. The image of my mother walking into that bathroom broke me more than the heat ever could.

Attempt 4: If at first you don't succeed, try, try again. I googled the least evasive way to commit suicide and the response was carbon monoxide poisoning and doing so should only take five to six minutes.

I walked into the garage quietly, not angry, not dramatic, just empty.

Empty is more dangerous than rage.

I started the car. Closed the door. Laid down beneath the tailpipes with a Goodwill bag as a pillow.

There was no music playing. No tears streaming. Just stillness.

After an hour of inhaling fumes, my phone rang. I felt it. Then it rang again. And again. I finally answered.

A voice said: "I felt it in my spirit that something was wrong. Dying like this will kill your mama slowly." It was Conquistador, a good friend who called me repeatedly and I didn't answer until he made his number show up private, and that's when I answered. "Don't do this. Not like this. If you died any other way like natural causes, she would be able to handle it. Don't do this. Not like this."

It broke something—or maybe it saved something. Either way, it pulled me out of that garage alive.

I didn't leave healed. I left rescued. Rescue is messy. It's not triumphant. It's shaky hands and burning lungs and tears you didn't know were there.

Shaking and overwhelmed, I knew I couldn't hold the truth inside anymore. I called my daddy. He was at church, but he answered. Through tears, the only word I could get out was suicide.

He thought I meant I was thinking about it—not that I had already attempted it 4 different times in the past 24 hours. His voice was stern but loving: "Don't you ever think about doing anything like that. I know you're trying to get back on your feet, but your family—we are here to help you."

Sometimes the voice of a father sounds like command and compassion in the same breath.

As I listened, Kurt Carr's lyrics wrapped around my heart: "I almost let go … I felt like I just couldn't take life anymore. My problems had me bound, depression weighed me down …" And then the line that saved me: "But God held me close, so I wouldn't let go."

And He did. God held me through the pain, the confusion, the shame, the attempts, the darkness that tried to swallow me whole.

That day became my SSDI onset date—but more importantly, it became the day heaven said, "This one will live and declare My works."

Not because I was strong. Not because I was disciplined. But because mercy interrupted me.

I almost let go . . . but God held me close. And that is why He kept me.

WHAT THIS MEANS FOR YOUR LIFE

This is the chapter where I stop being an author and start being a witness.

If you are reading this and you have ever thought about ending your life, I need you to hear me: **Depression is a liar. And the lie it tells best is that your death would be a gift to the people you love.**

I believed that lie on November 26, 2023. I believed my life insurance would pay off my house. I believed my family would be better off without the burden of my existence. I believed my death would be more valuable than my life.

That is the most dangerous lie depression tells. Because it takes your love for others—the best part of you—and weaponizes it against you.

Let me name six lies depression tells so you can recognize them before they become decisions:

Lie 1: "Everyone would be better off without you." Truth: The people who love you would be devastated. Conquistador told me, "Dying like this will kill your mama slowly." He was right. My death would not have freed my family; it would have imprisoned them in grief.

Lie 2: "You are a burden." Truth: You are not a burden. You are carrying a burden. There is a difference. Burdens can be shared. Burdens can be lightened. You are a person worthy of help.

Lie 3: "This pain will never end." Truth: Pain is temporary, even when it doesn't feel like it. I have survived November 26, 2023. I am here. The pain shifted. It always does.

Lie 4: "Nobody understands." Truth: People do understand. Millions of people have fought this same battle. You are not alone—you have just been isolated. Isolation is the enemy's territory. Community is God's.

Lie 5: "You've gone too far to come back." Truth: You haven't. You are reading this book. You are still here. And "still here" is all God needs to start the next chapter.

Lie 6: "The places that should help you won't." Truth: When I asked my church for financial help after tithing faithfully since 1993 and was told they had a one-time policy, it felt like the final door slamming shut. Depression used that moment to whisper, "See? Even the church doesn't care." But that was not God's voice. That was a policy. God's provision has never been limited to one institution, one system, or one door. When one door closes, God opens a window—and sometimes He tears the whole wall down. Do not let one institution's limitations become your definition of God's capacity.

If you are in crisis right now: Call or text 988. That's it. Three numbers. Someone will answer. Someone will listen. Your call is free, confidential, and immediate.

APPLY THIS

- If you have ever had suicidal thoughts, tell one person. A therapist. A pastor. A friend. A family member. Break the silence today.
- If you know someone who is struggling, call them. Don't text. Call. Conquistador called me repeatedly until I answered. That phone call saved my life.
- Remove the phrase "they're just being dramatic" from your vocabulary. When someone expresses despair, believe them.
- If you are a church leader, review your benevolence policies. A one-time assistance limit may protect a budget, but it can devastate a member who has been faithfully sowing for decades. The church should be the last place someone feels abandoned. Ask yourself: if a faithful member came to us in their darkest hour, would our policy reflect the heart of Christ—or the heart of an institution?
- If your church turned you away in your time of need, grieve it. Name it. But do not let it define your relationship with God. God's faithfulness is not measured by the faithfulness of any single church. Seek community that matches your commitment—and if it doesn't exist, be the one who builds it.

IF YOU'RE IN A GROUP

- Have you ever believed 1 of the 6 lies Thoris names? Which one resonated most?
- Conquistador's phone call saved Thoris's life. What does that teach us about the power of showing up—even when it feels intrusive?
- How can we create spaces in our churches and communities where people feel safe enough to say, "I'm not okay"?
- Thoris tithed faithfully for over thirty years, and when he asked his church for financial help, he was told they had a one-time policy. How should churches balance financial stewardship with caring for members in crisis? What would you want your church to do differently?
- Have you ever felt abandoned by an institution you gave your time, money, or trust to? How did that experience shape your faith—and how did you separate God from the institution?

If you or someone you know is struggling with thoughts of suicide, please call or text 988 to reach the Suicide & Crisis Lifeline. Help is available 24/7.

Help is available.

If you're having thoughts of self-harm or suicide, call or text 988, or chat via the Suicide & Crisis Lifeline. You will reach someone trained to listen.

It's free. It's confidential. It's immediate.

Prayer: Father God, thank you for keeping me when I tried to let go. Thank you for the phone call, the interruption, the mercy that arrived when I had nothing left. For every person reading this who has wondered if their death would be a gift—speak louder than the lie. Tell them the truth: their life is needed, their breath is rebellion against darkness, and You are not finished with them yet. In Jesus's name. Amen.

What I describe in this chapter is my own experience, not a diagnosis or a treatment plan. If any of it sounds like your life, please talk to a mental-health professional—and if you are in danger right now, call or text 988. —T.

"Sometimes the darkest place becomes the doorway where God pulls you back into the light."

CHAPTER 18

APRIL 19, 2024—THE DAY THAT CHANGED EVERYTHING

Written by Thoris Lamar Burt

"The Lord is close to the brokenhearted and saves those who are crushed in spirit."

PSALM 34:18 (NIV)

There are days that tap you on the shoulder . . . and then there are days that crack the earth open beneath your feet. April 19, 2024, was that day for me.

It did not arrive with warning. It did not knock politely. It came heavy. Sacred. Terrifying. Necessary. It was the day my mama underwent major lumbar spinal surgery at AdventHealth South—the day God said, "This is where healing begins—for both of you."

Hospitals have a smell you never forget. A mixture of antiseptic, fear, and fragile hope. That morning, as they wheeled her away, I felt like a little boy again—helpless, praying, trying to be strong while my insides trembled.

When Mama opened her eyes after surgery, I was the first person she saw—standing right by her side, just like she did for me when I was a child. And in that moment, the roles reversed without either of us announcing it. Just 11 days earlier, on April 8, 2024, I received a six-figure job offer while taking her to a doctor's appointment. We both shouted and cried with joy. Mama told me she was proud of me—something I didn't hear often growing up. That sentence landed deeper than the salary.

I always felt like she resented me for not finishing college, but school wasn't for me. After making real money at the age of twenty-one, I knew my path was different. Still, there is something about wanting your mother's affirmation—even as a grown man—that never fades.

Later that night, I sensed my mama crying. I've always had that gift—even as a child. I could feel her tears long before I could ever hear them. It is strange how trauma sharpens certain senses. When you grow up navigating tension, you learn how to detect shifts in energy. You learn to feel pain before it speaks. When I was a boy, I'd often feel a tug in my spirit and walk into the room—and I'd find her crying because her boyfriend was drunk and arguing with her. That same tug woke me up that night after her surgery.

I checked on her, and she told me they were tears of joy—joy that the excruciating pain was gone, and joy that I had been by her side nonstop since surgery.

But there was more behind those tears. She told me something that shook me: "God told me He delayed your job and He kept you from your suicide attempts because He needed you here with me at my most vulnerable time." That sentence rearranged my entire understanding of suffering.

She looked at me and said, "As long as I'm alive, YOU will NEVER suffer again."

That wasn't just a mother speaking; that was a covenant forming in real time. She told me God placed it on her heart to help me start my new job with a clean slate financially. I told her she didn't have to do that—that I was there out of love, not out of need. But she insisted. Because when a mother sees the edge her child almost stepped off of, money becomes insignificant compared to preservation. She said she finally knew which of her children would show up for her when it mattered—even though people inside and outside our family labeled me crazy or unstable.

That part stung. Because while I was battling schizoaffective disorder, fighting thoughts that tried to take me out, some people reduced me to a diagnosis. But she saw something different that day. She remembered the day I shared my bill spreadsheet and passwords with her and my daddy—preparing them to handle my affairs because I didn't think I'd survive my mental health battle. That wasn't theatrics; that was planning for departure. I wasn't being dramatic. I was planning. My life insurance policies were beyond the suicide exclusion period. I believed I was leaving a legacy. I thought I was being responsible. I thought I was being strategic. I thought I was easing their burden.

But God said, "Not yet. I'm not done with you."

Mama's transfers from one health facility to another told a story: April 22, 2024, to AdventHealth Winter Park. May 1, 2024, to The Mayflower. Each shift was more than a facility change—it was a shift in our relationship.

Winter Park was clinical. The Mayflower was reflective. In between therapy sessions and medication schedules, walls began to fall. God used hospital rooms, rehab hallways, and vulnerable nights to heal broken places in both of us.

We talked—not just about logistics, but about wounds. We cried—not out of fear, but out of release. We forgave—not selectively, but fully. We listened—not to defend, but to understand.

There were conversations we should have had years earlier. There were apologies that finally found language. There were fears that finally met compassion.

And somewhere between Winter Park Hospital and The Mayflower, something holy happened: This book was born.

It wasn't polished. It wasn't strategic. It was raw.

It was two people deciding that pain would not have the final word.

It was Mama's idea. She said, "We need to tell what God has done."

So right there—in hospital chairs, rehab common rooms, and late-night conversations—we started writing.

Writing became therapy. Writing became testimony. Writing became survival.

WHAT THIS MEANS FOR YOUR LIFE

My mama said something in that hospital that rearranged my entire theology of suffering: "God told me He delayed your job and He kept you from your suicide attempts because He needed you here with me at my most vulnerable time."

Read that again.

God delayed a blessing so I could be in position for an assignment.

If you are waiting for something—a job, a relationship, a breakthrough, a healing—and you cannot understand why it hasn't come yet, consider this: **The delay may not be about you at all. It may be about someone else who needs you exactly where you are right now.**

Your waiting season might be someone else's answered prayer.

APPLY THIS

- Reframe your waiting. Instead of asking "Why hasn't God answered yet?" ask "Who needs me right here, right now?"
- Look for the assignment in the delay. Who in your immediate circle is going through something that requires your presence? Show up for them this week.
- Write down one delay in your life that you later realized was divine timing. Let that memory anchor your faith during current seasons of waiting.

IF YOU'RE IN A GROUP

- Has there ever been a time when something you were waiting for was delayed—and you later realized the delay served someone else?
- Thoris's mama said, "As long as I'm alive, YOU will NEVER suffer again." What is the most powerful thing a parent has ever spoken over your life?
- How does the idea that "your waiting season might be someone else's answered prayer" change the way you view difficult seasons?

April 19, 2024, didn't just change her body. It changed our family. It changed our story. It changed me. It forced me to confront the fact that I was still here for a reason. Sometimes God lets everything fall apart . . . so He can show you what He's been holding together the whole time. And sometimes the day that almost breaks you . . . becomes the day that rebuilds you.

Prayer: Father God, thank you for the days that change everything. Thank you for delays I once resented that turned out to be divine timing. Where I am still waiting on something, help me see the assignment in the season. Teach me that my waiting may be someone else's answered prayer and let me show up faithfully right where You've placed me. In Jesus's name. Amen.

"Some days break you open,

not to destroy you—but to

let the healing light in."

PART VI

RESTORING: SIGNS, SYMBOLS, AND THE ROAD BACK

Core Teaching: God restores in layers—mind, body, and the bonds we thought were broken for good.

CHAPTER 19

SIGNS AND SYMBOLS IN ROOM 235

Written by Thoris Lamar Burt

"The person without the Spirit does not accept the things that come from the Spirit of God but considers them foolishness, and cannot understand them because they are discerned only through the Spirit."

1 CORINTHIANS 2:14 (NIV)

Some places leave no mark on you, and then there are places like Room 235—rooms that don't just exist in time but carve themselves into your soul. I didn't walk into Room 235 expecting revelation. I didn't expect God to speak. I didn't expect healing to begin where fear had settled. But that's the thing about God—He rarely schedules miracles. He simply steps in.

Room 235 at The Mayflower was supposed to be a temporary space for Mama's recovery after her transfer from Advent Health. It was supposed to be functional, quiet, ordinary. But from the moment

I stepped inside, something in that room felt different. The air felt thick with meaning, like God had left fingerprints all over the walls.

Even before I noticed the paintings, the signs were already there.

The first physical therapist assigned to evaluate my mama upon her arrival at The Mayflower was named **Armando.** At first, I didn't think much of it. But later that evening, when I briefly went home to shower and gather clothes, I pulled into my driveway and saw my own address printed across the mailbox:

9901 Armando Circle.

Armando.

Same name. Same spelling. Same season.

It stopped me.

It felt like God whispering, *You are not here by accident. Healing isn't confined to a building—it follows you home.*

Then there was **Tracy**—one of the staff members assisting with my mama's care. Her name was spelled exactly the same as my sister's: Tracy.

And that detail pierced deeper than coincidence.

My sister Tracy had stopped speaking to Mama on Mother's Day 2023. Now, during this season in rehab at The Mayflower in Winter Park, we were approaching the one-year anniversary of that silence.

And here was a Tracy—in a place of healing—helping care for our mother.

God had placed the name back in the room.

As if reconciliation was being rehearsed in the Spirit before it ever manifested in reality.

And then there was **Jessica.**

Jessica was the only Black CNA at The Mayflower. Her name was spelled exactly the same as my first cousin—my mama's niece—Uncle Henry's daughter.

Same spelling. Same familiarity. Same grounding presence.

Out of all the staff, the only Black CNA—the one whose presence immediately felt culturally safe and spiritually steady—carried the same name as family.

It was as if God kept embedding reminders in plain sight:

You are not alone. Family still surrounds you. Even when relationships are strained, I will surround you with echoes of connection.

At first, I brushed off the feeling. After everything I'd been through—the depression, the anxiety, the trauma of my initial mental episode on April 29, 2018 and the garage on November 26, 2023—I thought maybe I was just overwhelmed. Maybe I was imagining things. Maybe my spirit was trying to make sense of too much pain in too little time.

Even the automatic bathroom lights unsettled me at first.

The lights in the bathroom of Room 235 were motion-activated. Yet more than once, they flipped on without anyone walking toward the doorway. I remember staring at the door, wondering if the sensors were malfunctioning. My mind, already sensitive and hyperaware, started trying to interpret what I was seeing.

For a split second, I questioned everything.

But then something grounded me.

Mama has always slept with her hall light on near the bathroom next to my old room. She sleeps in my old bedroom a lot, and that bathroom is the one she prefers because the walk-in shower is larger. From as far back as I remember in that house, I've known that light stays on—a quiet glow in the hallway through the night.

The light wasn't eerie. It was familiar. It was comfort. It was routine.

In that moment, God reminded me: Not every light turning on is a mystery. Sometimes it's just comfort echoing what you've always known. The signs weren't chaos; they were reassurance.

And then came May 8.

Looking back, I can see the signs were there even that morning. Before the day unfolded a way none of us wanted. There were signs that morning—subtle, almost laughable in isolation, but heavy in hindsight.

Earlier in the workplace, before the mental fog fully consumed me, in the middle of a conversation with Steve Stricker—someone I had worked with at Cogent Communications and previously at Windstream, he looked at me and said, "Cold hands = warm heart."

He had said it before. But that day, it landed differently. Because my mama has always said the same thing about me—that my hands are always cold. From the time I was young, she would grab them and say, "Your hands stay cold, but you've got a warm heart."

And there I was, in the morning of May 8, 2024, hearing the same phrase again.

Cold hands. Warm heart.

At the time, I didn't pause long enough to process it. But looking back, I see it as another whisper in plain sight. Another reminder that even when my mind felt unstable, even when fear was creeping in, even when the fog was beginning to thicken—my heart was still intact.

My illness was loud, but my heart was still warm. The signs that day weren't just in Room 235. They were in the names. In the numbers. In the timing. In the light. In the coldness of my hands. In the warmth of words spoken casually by someone who had no idea he was echoing my mother.

God was layering reassurance before the storm fully broke.

But then I started to see.

There were paintings on the wall—abstract at first glance, but intentional in their arrangement. Soft blues, deep greens, strokes of gold, gentle spirals that looked like movement, like breath, like resurrection. The more I stared, the more something inside me stirred.

I didn't know what I was looking at. Not fully. But my spirit knew before my mind understood.

WHAT THIS MEANS FOR YOUR LIFE

This is a chapter that requires discernment to teach and discernment to receive.

I saw signs—in names, numbers, paintings, and timing—that felt like God speaking to me. My mentor confirmed it. My spirit recognized it. But I also live with a condition that can produce hallucinations and paranoia.

So how do you tell the difference between divine communication and mental distortion?

Here are three tests I use:

Test 1: Does it align with Scripture? God will never communicate something that contradicts His Word. If what you're perceiving leads you toward fear, isolation, paranoia, or harm, it is not from God. If it leads toward healing, reconciliation, peace, and hope, it may well be.

Test 2: Does it produce fruit or chaos? The signs in Room 235 produced healing between my mama and me. They produced clarity. They produced this book. Good fruit. If what you're perceiving produces chaos, confusion, or relational damage, step back and consult a trusted spiritual mentor and a mental health professional.

Test 3: Can someone else see it? My mentor saw the paintings without prompting. He identified the symbols independently. When God is speaking, often He confirms it through other people. If you are the only person who can see what you're seeing, seek confirmation before you build on it.

APPLY THIS

- If you believe God is speaking to you through signs or circumstances, apply the three tests above before acting on what you perceive.
- Find a trusted spiritual mentor you can talk to about what you're experiencing. Not someone who will just agree with you—someone who will help you discern.
- If you live with a mental health condition, work with your therapist to distinguish between spiritual experiences and symptoms. Both can be real. Both deserve attention. But they require different responses.

IF YOU'RE IN A GROUP

- How do you personally discern between God speaking and your own mind creating meaning?
- Thoris's mentor confirmed what he was sensing. Why is community important in spiritual discernment?
- How can we honor someone's spiritual experiences without dismissing their mental health reality—and vice versa?

Prayer: Father God, give me discernment that aligns with Your Word, confirms through trusted voices, and produces good fruit in my life. Protect me from confusion and from believing every impression my mind manufactures. Speak to me clearly, Lord, in ways I can recognize—and surround me with people who help me test what I perceive. In Jesus's name. Amen.

"God speaks in patterns, names, and numbers. Discernment is learning the difference between His voice and your fear. Some rooms hold more than memories—they hold messages only the Spirit can translate... and sometimes, they hold light that turns on before you even know you need it."

CHAPTER 20

HE NEVER LEFT MY SIDE

Written by Carolyn Virginia Burt

"So do not fear, for I am with you; do not be dismayed,
for I am your God. I will strengthen you and help you;
I will uphold you with my righteous right hand."

ISAIAH 41:10 (NIV)

On April 19, 2024, I underwent spinal surgery on my lumbar vertebrae L4 and L5 at AdventHealth on Rollins Avenue. The surgery was intended to resolve the severe sciatic pain that had radiated from my buttocks down to my feet for over a year.

When I woke up from anesthesia, the excruciating pain I had lived with for so long was gone—by the grace of God.

The very first person I saw was my son, Thoris. He had never left my side.

Just six hours after surgery, with the assistance of a physical therapist, I was able to stand and walk; that alone felt like a miracle.

My secondary rehabilitation began at AdventHealth Winter Park, where I worked on regaining coordination in my hands, legs, and feet. Every clinician involved in my recovery journey was exceptional, and I remain deeply grateful for the care I received.

The unconditional time Thoris spent with me throughout my surgery and rehabilitation was truly a blessing. He asked questions I would not have even thought to ask—especially while I was still under the effects of anesthesia. His presence ensured that I was not only cared for but also advocated for.

My final rehabilitation placement was The Mayflower in Winter Park, Florida, where I arrived on May 1, 2024. During our time there, Thoris and I were able to address many things we had brushed under the rug over the years—conversations that had been hurtful, unresolved, or avoided. Though difficult, those moments brought clarity and truth between us.

On May 8, 2024, my phone was lying on the bed beside me in Room 235. Thoris walked into the room, picked up my phone, and told me not to answer it. He said that artificial intelligence was listening to our calls and insisted that I should not answer—even if my son Terrell called.

I was terrified by the way Thoris was behaving. I did not understand what AI was or what he was talking about. Thoris was extremely paranoid and believed something terrible was going to happen. I started crying hysterically because I didn't understand why he wouldn't give me my phone or let me talk to anyone. I felt like my lifeline was being taken from me.

During this time, Thoris called two of my friends—one in Alabama and one in Orlando. He questioned one of them about a previous conversation between us to test whether they could remember it, trying to determine if they were AI or real. The other he interrogated, asking them if they were truly my friend.

One could not remember the conversation about inviting me to Alabama after I was released from The Mayflower. The other denied being my friend. This further escalated Thoris's episode and his belief that AI had taken over my phone.

While I was crying, a nurse came into the room and asked if everything was okay. Thoris told her everything was fine and that she was not needed. I was crying so hard that I couldn't respond before she left.

Shortly afterward, police arrived with a nurse manager. The police told Thoris, "We're not going to hurt you. We just want to talk." Thoris replied respectfully, "Yes sir."

The nurse manager escorted me out of the room while the officers questioned Thoris. At that time, Thoris still had possession of my phone and personal items.

After the officers finished questioning him, the nurse manager went back into the room and requested my phone and personal items. Thoris initially refused. He said he wanted to see me and make sure I was okay, and he preferred to personally give me my phone and belongings to ensure I received them.

She returned and told me what he said, so I asked her to tell him, "Please give me my phone and personal items." When she made the request again, he gave them to her.

At that point, Thoris remained in Room 235 alone. To my knowledge, he was not disruptive or causing any issues. A nurse requested that Thoris leave, and he replied, "I'm not leaving until I see my mama and make sure she's okay."

The nurse advised him that I did not want to see him at that time. Thoris remained adamant that he needed to see me before he left.

This resulted in another call to police—this time, to serve a trespassing warning. When those officers arrived, they were not as pleasant as the first. They told him if he did not leave, he would be arrested. So, he complied—because that is what I taught him from a very young age. I taught him to respect law enforcement, and he had been around officers regularly when he was a child because of my work at Alabama A&M University.

Thoris did not understand why he was labeled as a trespasser. He was my caregiver and had orchestrated my stay at The Mayflower. The staff knew this. They had even provided a bed for him overnight because he was staying with me 24/7 until he started his new job, making sure I had the best care possible.

But due to his episode and the events leading up to the second set of officers being called, this became the outcome.

Even then, I know this truth: My son never left my side—until he was forced to.

WHAT THIS MEANS FOR YOUR LIFE

Caregiving is one of the most spiritually significant roles a person can play—and one of the least discussed in the church. If you are caring for a parent, a spouse, or a child through illness, surgery, or mental health crisis, this is for you:

You are not just running errands and scheduling appointments. You are ministering. Your presence is prayer in action. The questions you ask that they wouldn't think to ask—that is advocacy. The night you spend in a hospital chair—that is worship.

But caregiving also has a cost. If you do not care for yourself, you will break under the weight of caring for someone else. Rest is not selfish. Asking for help is not weakness. Setting boundaries is not betrayal.

APPLY THIS

- If you are currently caregiving, identify one thing you need this week that you have not asked for. Then ask for it.
- Accept that you cannot do everything alone. Identify one person who can share part of the load—even temporarily.
- Schedule one hour this week that is exclusively for your own restoration. Not errands. Not tasks. Rest.

IF YOU'RE IN A GROUP

- Carolyn describes watching her son care for her during her most vulnerable moment. What does it look like when roles reverse between parent and child?
- How do you maintain your own health while caring for someone else?

- Why does the church often celebrate caregiving without addressing the toll it takes?

Prayer: Father God, thank you for the ministry of presence. Thank you for the caregivers who show up without applause and serve without recognition. Strengthen them, Lord. Restore what their service has cost them. Where they have poured out, refill them. Where they have grown weary, carry them. Remind them that their presence is one of the most sacred forms of worship. In Jesus's name. Amen.

"Presence is ministry. Showing up is worship. The night you spend in a hospital chair is sacred ground. When healing began in my body, God was already revealing the strength He had been building in my son."

CHAPTER 21

TEARS OF JOY

Written by Thoris Lamar Burt

"Those who sow with tears will reap with songs of joy."

PSALM 126:5 (NIV)

On Sunday, May 5, 2024, somewhere between 3 and 4 in the quiet hours before dawn, I woke up with tears already sliding down my face. Not the frantic tears of panic. Not the empty tears of depression. These tears were warm . . . steady . . . holy. They felt like something inside me had finally unclenched—like my soul had been holding its breath for months and had finally decided to exhale.

For so long, my tears had been warnings. Signals. Alarms sounding from the darker corners of my mind. But these? These tears didn't break me. They lifted me. They felt like God had slipped into the room while I slept and touched a part of me I didn't even know needed touching.

Then my phone buzzed. It was a devotional from my brother Jeremy, who has become the spiritual anchor of our family. Every day, he sends us devotionals—seeds he plants, never knowing which one will bloom at the right moment. That morning, the topic was tears. How tears aren't always the evidence of pain, but the manifestation of divine awareness. Awareness of God's presence, God's mercy, God's fingerprints still on your life.

When I read it, something inside me broke wide open—but beautifully this time. Quietly. With peace instead of fear. Because the truth was simple and impossible to ignore: I was still here.

After all I'd lived through—four suicide attempts, the time in the garage with the engine running and no will to live, a heart blockage, a divorce that gutted me, layoffs, spiritual droughts, family tensions, nights when my mind turned into a battlefield I was losing… I'd woken up. I'd survived. I didn't die in my despair. My story didn't end in the garage. My life didn't conclude on a cold hospital bed. My purpose didn't collapse with my marriage. God carried me through every moment when I was unable to carry myself.

And that realization? It hit me with the softness of a whisper but the strength of a tidal wave: This is what it meant to be *kept*.

No dramatic signs. No lightning. No booming voice from the clouds. Just a sunrise-on-the-inside moment where my heart finally understood that God had been holding me in every shadow, covering me in every breakdown, redirecting me every time I tried to walk away from my future.

I thought about the days leading up to that moment—Mama's spinal surgery and the transfers from facility to facility. What felt like a vision of what was to come of the May 8th crisis at The Mayflower, where I spiraled again . . . (And my brother Terrell *just happened* to be there at the exact moment I needed him—a coincidence I know was divine!)

The trained crisis officers who treated me like a human being, not a problem. The untrained officers who arrived later, escalating things—yet God still covered me and got me home safely in a fog I barely remember.

That was not luck. That was not coincidence. That was not randomness. That was God. Keeping me. Shielding me. Intercepting destruction.

So, when joy returned to me on that early Sunday morning, it didn't shout. It whispered. It settled. It wrapped itself around me like a warm blanket in a cold room and said, "I never left you. You just stopped feeling Me."

Those tears weren't sorrow—they were prophecy. Evidence that the seeds I sowed in the darkest chapters of my life were finally beginning to bloom. Evidence that Psalm 126:5 was no longer just a verse . . . it was my life.

Joy didn't come back with fireworks. It came back with understanding. With breath. With stillness. With awareness that even when I lost hope in myself, God never lost hope in me.

And that's why this moment matters. Because joy doesn't just return—joy remembers. Joy revisits the places where pain once lived and says, "Let me show you what God was doing behind the scenes."

On that Sunday morning, I realized something I will never forget: My tears were not the evidence of defeat—they were the evidence of preservation.

This is what it means to be kept. Not spared from storms—but held through them. Not protected from battles—but strengthened to survive them. Not saved from tears—but promised joy on the other side.

I didn't just wake up crying that morning. I woke up reborn.

WHAT THIS MEANS FOR YOUR LIFE

Joy after trauma is not denial; it is a miracle.

When you have survived what should have destroyed you, and joy returns—do not question it. Do not feel guilty for smiling. Do not wonder if you deserve it.

Joy doesn't erase sorrow. It redeems it. Those tears on May 5, 2024, were evidence that the seeds I sowed in the darkest chapters of my life were finally beginning to bloom.

If you are in a dark season right now and joy feels impossible, hold on to Psalm 126:5: "Those who sow with tears will reap with songs of joy." That is a promise. Not a suggestion. Not a possibility. A promise.

Your morning is coming. And when it arrives, let it come without apology.

APPLY THIS

- If joy feels distant, write down one thing you are grateful for today. Just one. Do this for seven consecutive days. Gratitude is the doorway joy walks through.

- Give yourself permission to feel good. If you've been through trauma and you're starting to smile again, that is not disloyalty to your pain. That is evidence of healing.
- Send a message to someone who helped you survive your dark season. Tell them what they meant to you. Joy multiplies when it is shared.

IF YOU'RE IN A GROUP

- Have you ever felt guilty for experiencing joy after a season of suffering? Why?
- Thoris describes waking up with tears of joy after years of tears of pain. What would that moment mean to you?
- How do you distinguish between joy and denial?

Prayer: Lord, thank you for every tear that watered the soil of my healing. Thank you for meeting me in my lowest valleys and lifting me into joy I didn't think I would feel again. Keep my heart open, my spirit sensitive, and my steps aligned with Your grace. Amen.

"Joy doesn't always shout—

sometimes it slips in softly,

sits beside your sorrow, and

says, 'I'm still here."

CHAPTER 22

WHEN TRAINING MEETS THE MOMENT

Written by Thoris Lamar Burt

"The righteous cry, and the Lord heareth, and delivereth them out of all their troubles."

PSALM 34:17

There are some seasons you look back on and realize God was working way before you even knew you were in danger.

That's how it feels when I look at April 29, 2018, November 26, 2023, May 8, 2024, and May 4, 2025.

Four different days.

Four different breakdowns.

Four different versions of me.

And four different responses from the system that was supposed to help me.

To understand why those dates matter, you have to zoom out beyond Orlando, beyond Florida, and look at the bigger story of how police and mental health ever got forced into the same room.

Years ago, in another city, a man in the middle of a mental-health crisis crossed paths with officers who didn't understand what they were seeing. They had badges, guns, and authority—but no training on psychosis, bipolar episodes, or suicidal ideation. It ended in a death that could have been avoided if someone in the room had been equipped to see illness instead of just *noncompliance*.

That tragedy sparked what later became known as Crisis Intervention Team training—CIT. A simple but powerful idea: teach officers how to recognize a mental-health crisis, how to slow down instead of speed up, how to use their words before their weapons, and how to get people to treatment instead of just into handcuffs.

Over time, that model spread. Different states and cities adopted pieces of it, creating teams of officers specifically trained to respond when the 911 call wasn't about a crime, but a crisis.

Florida eventually joined that movement. Agencies across the state began sending officers through specialized training so that when they encountered someone in the middle of a breakdown, they could respond with understanding instead of fear. It wasn't perfect. It wasn't everywhere. But it was a start.

Orlando would later take it a step further with something called the Community Response Team—CRT. Instead of just sending officers, they created a unit that brought a licensed clinician, a paramedic, and a specially trained officer together on mental-health calls. It was an acknowledgment that some emergencies are medical and emotional before they are anything else.

When I experienced my very first mental episode in 2018, CRT didn't exist yet.

Back then, when things in my mind started to slip, the only option was regular patrol officers. They didn't have a clinician riding with them. They didn't have behavioral health embedded in their unit. They didn't have the depth of training that would later become standard.

So, when they responded to me, they saw behavior without context. They saw a situation to manage, not a person to understand. I didn't walk away from that encounter feeling helped. I walked away feeling ashamed. It taught me a dangerous lesson: that reaching out during a breakdown might make things worse, not better.

I carried that wound into the years that followed.

By the time we get to November 26, 2023, a different kind of weight had piled up on top of that early experience—job loss, financial pressure, family distance, church hurt, and the quiet, suffocating whisper that maybe my life was more of a burden than a blessing.

But God stepped in through a voice on the other end of a phone call, through a reminder of my mother's heart, through lyrics I'd heard years before that suddenly became a lifeline. He pulled me out of that garage alive.

I didn't walk out healed. I walked out rescued.

What I didn't realize in that moment was that God wasn't just keeping me from dying that day—He was keeping me long enough for something else to catch up: the system.

By the time I got to May 8, 2024, at The Mayflower in Winter Park, a different structure was in place. CIT had been launched, and CIT-trained officers existed. Mental-health awareness inside the department had grown. My brother was aware and he advocated for the kind of response I needed.

On that day, when my mind slipped again and I went into another episode, the first set of officers who arrived were CIT-trained.

The difference was immediate: their presence was calm; their voices were steady; their questions were gentle but clear.

They spoke to me like I was an overwhelmed human being—not a criminal, not a problem, not a threat. They didn't just react to my behavior; they tried to understand the pain underneath it.

For a moment, I felt seen.

But then a second set of officers—who were not trained the same way—came into the picture, and the tone shifted. The energy got colder. The interaction became more about control and procedure and less about understanding. The way they spoke to me, the decisions they made, and the harsh way they handled me left a mark.

The only reason that day didn't spiral into something worse is because the first contact I had was with those CIT-trained officers—the ones who treated me with dignity when I was at my lowest.

That's the contrast that haunts me and comforts me at the same time. It haunts me because it shows how easily things can go wrong when the wrong people, with the wrong training, show up first. It comforts me because it proves that training and compassion are not abstract ideas—they are life and death.

Fast forward to May 4, 2025, I experienced another crisis. I was having visual, auditory, and tactile hallucinations. I hadn't slept. I couldn't reach my psychiatrist. So, I did something a lot of people are afraid to do—I called the police on myself.

This moment was captured by my doorbell camera. These CIT-trained officers—Crisis Intervention Team officers—escorted me out of my home to get medical attention. No handcuffs. No aggression. No weapons drawn. Just six officers trained to treat a mental health crisis like what it is—a medical emergency.

When I look back at 2018, I can see so clearly how CRT could have changed that moment. If a clinician had been on scene, they would have recognized symptoms, not just *behavior*. If a paramedic had been present, they could have focused on my safety, not just my compliance. If a crisis-trained officer had been there with that team, they could have guided the situation with calmness instead of confusion.

My first encounter with the system didn't come with those tools. So, I walked away with trauma instead of trust.

But God, in His timing, allowed me to live long enough that by the time the next storms hit—November 26, 2023, May 8, 2024, and May 4, 2025—the world around me had more to offer than it did in

2018. There were better officers, better models, better partnerships, and better language for what I was going through.

God didn't just keep me on November 26, 2023. He kept me through 2018. He kept me into 2024, 2025, and I'm still kept. He kept me until CIT existed in my city. He kept me until my family knew how to advocate for me and for me to advocate for myself. He kept me until help had more hands, more wisdom, and more heart.

My survival is not just about what God did in my spirit. It's also about how He moved in policies, training rooms, city budgets, and department cultures—long before I ever fell apart.

That's why this chapter belongs in this book. Because when I say, "Why HE kept me," I'm not just talking about Him keeping my heart beating. I'm talking about Him aligning systems, officers, clinicians, paramedics, advocates, and family members so that when I broke, there was something in place to catch me.

Not perfectly. Not painlessly. But enough to keep me here. Enough for me to tell this story.

WHAT THIS MEANS FOR YOUR LIFE

This chapter is a call to action for three groups of people:

For families with loved ones who have mental illness: Learn what crisis intervention resources exist in your city before you need them. Do you have a Community Response Team? Does your police department offer CIT-trained officers? Can you request them specifically when calling 911? Know these answers now. In a crisis, you will not have time to research.

For churches: You should be the safest place for someone having a mental health crisis—not the last place they'd go. Train your deacons, your elders, your pastors in Mental Health First Aid. Partner with local mental health organizations. Stop treating mental illness as a prayer-only problem and start treating it as a whole-person concern.

For the person who has had a negative experience with crisis response: Your trauma is valid. You deserved better. But do not let one bad experience prevent you from seeking help in the future. The system is imperfect, but it is improving. And God is sovereign over every system.

APPLY THIS

- Research your local crisis intervention resources today. Does your city have a CRT or CIT-trained officers? Write down the number.
- If you are a church leader, schedule a Mental Health First Aid training for your leadership team this year. Resources are available through NAMI and Mental Health First Aid USA.
- If you've had a negative experience with law enforcement during a mental health crisis, document it. Your story can help advocate for better training and policy changes.

IF YOU'RE IN A GROUP

- Thoris experienced both CIT-trained and untrained officers during different crises. What does that tell us about the importance of training?

- How can churches become first responders for mental health in their communities?
- What would change if every 911 call involving mental health automatically dispatched a clinician alongside officers?

Prayer: Father God, thank you for the people You position in my life before I even know I need them. For every CIT-trained officer, every clinician, every advocate who shows up in someone's worst moment with training and compassion—bless them, multiply them, and call more workers into that field. Make our churches the safest place for someone in crisis, not the last place they'd come. In Jesus's name. Amen.

"Some storms come to destroy you. Others come to reveal Who's been holding you together the whole time."

CHAPTER 23

THERAPY, TEARS, AND TRIUMPH—DEPRESSION IN SILENCE, ANXIETY IN MOTION

Written by Thoris Lamar Burt

"Weeping may stay for the night, but rejoicing comes in the morning."

PSALM 30:5 (NIV)

My therapy sessions have been stitched together with lessons, tears, and quiet triumphs—the kind of triumphs you don't brag about, but you feel deep in your bones. Healing isn't loud. Healing is ancient. It's that slow, steady rhythm your spirit remembers, even when your mind forgets.

But healing also has a way of dragging the truth into the light, and the truth ... well, it rarely shows up pretty.

I remember one session where my therapist asked me, gently but directly, "What was the moment you realized you wanted to live again?"

And immediately—without hesitation—my mind went to November 26, 2023. The garage. The closed door. The running engine. The darkness pressing in.

And the phone call from Conquistador—the one that broke through the fog and shattered the silence.

I told my therapist how he said, "Your mama would die slowly knowing you died that way." That sentence didn't just hit me—it snatched me back from the edge. When I shared that in therapy, I cried so hard I could barely catch my breath. Because that moment wasn't just a memory. It was a scar. A turning point. A resurrection.

My therapist didn't flinch. She held the space. She said, "That's the night you survived on purpose."

And she was right.

In another session, I told her about May 8th—the day at The Mayflower when I was in a mental fog so thick, I could barely tell up from down. I told her how Mama was recovering from spinal surgery, how Terrell just happened to be there, how the first set of officers treated me with compassion... but the second team walked in untrained and unprepared for a mental health crisis.

I told her how they handed me a trespass warning when I was in no state to understand anything. How I somehow drove home through that fog—a miracle in itself. And how the only explanation I have for surviving that drive is: BUT GOD.

My therapist paused and said, "Those moments could have destroyed you. But instead, they revealed you."

Those sessions—those raw, unfiltered confessions—became the place where I finally learned the difference between surviving and healing.

And then came the session about Mama. The one where I told my therapist how Mama looked at me and said she trusted me again—fully, openly, with that same warmth she had in the 90s when she was raising us up the best way she knew how.

I told my therapist how I showed up for Mama during the most vulnerable moment of her life: the surgery, the transfers, the setbacks, the worries. And Mama saw it. She felt it. She honored it. She said, "I know I can trust you again."

That sentence broke something open inside me—not in a way that wounded me, but in a way that healed what had been broken for years.

But therapy also made space for the practical side of healing. The bills. The stress. The weight. I didn't have the money to pay my car payment. I wasn't on the verge of repossession or foreclosure, but I was really struggling financially to keep up with my bills.

My therapist encouraged me to reach out to Lexus Financial and ask for help—something old-school pride would've never let me do. But healing requires humility. So, I called.

And when they granted me two months of waived payments, I felt like I could breathe again. Sometimes victory looks like survival. Sometimes it looks like a phone call. Sometimes it looks like God showing up through a customer service rep.

Then came the biggest triumph of all—the session where I shared how writing this book has been therapy in motion.

I told her how every chapter peels back another layer of who I am: the son, the survivor, the brother, the man who almost let go, the man God refused to let fall.

I told her how writing helps me understand my triggers, my stress points, my depressions, my anxieties, my cycles, and my strengths.

I told her how this book—this testimony—has become the place where I can finally see the purpose behind the pain.

This journey—from therapy to tears to triumph—is not a straight line. It loops, winds, dips, and climbs. It forces you to face the darkest parts of yourself and still choose light.

But every step leads me closer to the man God is shaping me to be.

Because yes, the night gets long. Yes, the tears get heavy. Yes, the memories sneak up without warning. Yes, the battles return when you least expect it.

But morning always comes. And when it comes? It doesn't knock softly. It bursts through like victory.

Depression has a way of slipping into your life without announcement—no knock at the door, no warning text, no slow fade-in. It just appears. It sits with you in the quiet moments, living in the spaces between your thoughts. It becomes the blanket you never asked for and the shadow you can't outrun. My depression has never been loud; it doesn't scream or demand attention. It shows up in silence—in the way I pull away from people I love, in the days when brushing my teeth feels like climbing a mountain, in the moments when I look alive on the outside but feel hollow on the inside.

There was a time when I mastered silence so well that people assumed I was fine. They thought my calm was peace when it was really exhaustion. They thought my smile was joy when it was really survival. Depression taught me how to blend in—how to make suffering look functional.

But anxiety . . . anxiety is a different beast. Where depression whispers, anxiety shouts. Where depression freezes, anxiety spins. My anxiety has always been in motion, like a storm behind my ribs. It makes me feel like I'm late even when I'm early. It turns rest into restlessness and sleep into battle. It sends my thoughts racing like they're trying to outrun my own heartbeat. Anxiety makes everything loud—the future, the past, the what-ifs, the almosts, the never-should-have-beens.

Both depression and anxiety shaped major events in my life—including the darkest night of my life on November 26, 2023. Sitting inside my garage with the engine running for over an hour—felt like surrender. I was ready not because I wanted to die, but because the pain felt louder than my hope.

And yet . . . in my silent depression and my anxious motion, God sent what I needed: a single phone call from Conquistador. A call he refused to stop making until I picked up. Depression may have wanted silence, but anxiety pushed me toward motion—and motion, in that moment, saved my life.

Months later, on May 8th at The Mayflower, anxiety took the wheel again—almost literally. I was in one of the worst mental fogs of my journey, barely aware of myself or my surroundings. I remember officers talking, forms being handed to me, voices blending together like static. I remember Mama recovering from surgery, Terrell showing up by what felt like divine appointment, and trained mental-health officers speaking to me with compassion. And then the untrained ones arrived—voices clipped, tone sharp, understanding absent. They handed me a trespass warning I don't even remember refusing. They let me drive home, even though my mind was somewhere else entirely.

When I told my therapist about that day, she stopped me mid-sentence and said, "Do you realize how dangerous that was? Driving in a mental fog is like driving blindfolded." I do realize it now. And still—BUT GOD. Because I made it home alive. Because my story didn't end on a quiet street in Winter Park. Because grace guarded the wheel when I couldn't.

Therapy helped me peel back the layers of what caused both the silence and the motion. We talked about childhood wounds, the pressure to be strong for everyone else, strong during my marriage for my wife and my nieces' sake, the nights when I held in my tears so no one would worry. We talked about my divorce—how the fear around my mental health played a part in my marriage collapsing. How even after doing everything right medically, a psychiatrist later explained something that could've changed the entire trajectory of my marriage: "You can still have mental episodes even when you take your medication exactly as prescribed."

That truth hit me like a freight train. For years, I carried the shame of a label I didn't deserve. For years, I thought my family feared me because I did something wrong. But it wasn't failure. It was biology. It was chemistry. It was misunderstanding. And therapy gave me permission to put that burden down.

We also discussed the Social Security Disability Insurance process—the long wait, the denials, the confusion, the emotional toll that comes with asking the system to believe your pain. Depression made the wait feel unbearable. Anxiety made every unknown feel like a threat. But when the approval finally came, it was like the first breath after being underwater too long.

One of the most healing moments came when Mama looked at me and said she trusted me again—fully, with no hesitation. That restored something in me I didn't even know was broken. Depression had convinced me I ruined that bond. Anxiety told me I had to earn it back. But love spoke louder than both.

Writing this book became another form of therapy. The silent parts of my depression found a voice on the page. The restless parts of my anxiety found a rhythm. Every chapter felt like exhaling after years of holding my breath. I learned things about myself I never noticed—patterns I never named, emotions I never processed.

My depression had depth. My anxiety had movement. My healing needed both.

Philippians 4:6–7 says God's peace will guard your heart and mind. That word "guard" hits differently when you've lived through battles of the mind. It means protection. It means covering. It means you are not fighting alone. It means even when your depression is quiet and your anxiety is loud—God stands watch.

Depression in silence. Anxiety in motion. Peace in the middle. I'm learning that healing isn't about erasing the past—it's about understanding it, honoring it, and rising from it with clarity. My mind has been both battlefield and sanctuary. Therapy helped me reclaim the ground I thought I lost.

And through every high, every low, every silent tear and every racing thought, God has guarded me with a peace that truly does transcend understanding.

"Sometimes the loudest battles happen in silence—but even silent battles can end in victory."

WHAT THIS MEANS FOR YOUR LIFE

Depression whispers. Anxiety screams. And most people have no idea which one they're dealing with—because both can look like "I'm fine" from the outside.

Let me give you a framework I wish someone had given me years ago:

Depression in Silence: Depression pulls inward. It makes you withdraw from people you love. It makes small tasks feel like mountains. It steals motivation, appetite, joy, and sleep. Depression doesn't always look like sadness. Sometimes it looks like numbness. Sometimes it looks like irritability. Sometimes it looks like a person who seems "fine" but has stopped caring about things they used to love.

Anxiety in Motion: Anxiety pushes outward. It makes you feel like you're running late even when you're early. It turns rest into restlessness. It sends your thoughts racing. Anxiety isn't just worry—it's your nervous system stuck in fight-or-flight mode, reacting to threats that may not exist.

Here are five signs you need to talk to someone:

- You've been unable to sleep—or unable to stop sleeping—for more than two weeks.
- You've lost interest in things that used to bring you joy.
- You've been having thoughts of self-harm or wishing you weren't alive.
- You can't stop the racing thoughts, no matter what you try.
- You've been isolating from people who love you without being able to explain why.

If any of those are true for you today, please hear me: **Therapy is not weakness. Therapy is wisdom.** I sit across from a therapist regularly, and those sessions have saved my life as much as any medication or prayer.

You do not have to choose between faith and therapy. God created both.

APPLY THIS

- If you recognized yourself in the description of depression or anxiety, schedule one appointment this week. A therapist, a doctor, a counselor. One appointment.
- Stop performing "I'm fine." The next time someone asks how you are, tell the truth. Even if the truth is, "I'm struggling."
- Write down your triggers—the situations, relationships, or environments that intensify your depression or anxiety. Knowing your triggers is the first step to managing them.

IF YOU'RE IN A GROUP

- Did you see yourself more in the description of depression or anxiety? Or both?
- Thoris says, "You do not have to choose between faith and therapy. God created both." How does that statement land for you?
- What would change in your church if therapy was discussed as openly as prayer?

Prayer: Father God, quiet the noise in my mind. Where depression has silenced my joy, speak hope. Where anxiety has stolen my rest, bring peace. Give me the courage to ask for help and the wisdom to know that seeking treatment honors You, not diminishes You. Guard my heart and mind in Christ Jesus. Amen.

> *What I describe in this chapter is my own experience, not a diagnosis or a treatment plan. If any of it sounds like your life, please talk to a mental-health professional—and if you are in danger right now, call or text 988. —T.*

"Some of my greatest breakthroughs were born from the tears I finally allowed myself to cry."

CHAPTER 24

FEAR ALMOST MADE ME LOSE MY SON

Written by Carolyn Virginia Burt

"For God has not given us a spirit of fear, but of power, love and of a sound mind."

2 TIMOTHY 1:7 (NIV)

This is one of the hardest chapters for me to write.

I took my own son to court.

And I did it because I was afraid.

After Thoris's mental health struggles and everything that happened, people began telling me stories. They said that people with mental illness kill their entire families. They said I needed to protect myself. They said I was in danger.

The more I listened, the more fear grew inside of me.

By July 2024—about a month after I was released from The Mayflower Rehab facility—my mind was not in a good place. The anesthesia from my surgery, the stress of recovery, and the constant voices of *friends* warning me had me in a terrified and paranoid state.

I left my home for eight days and went to Huntsville, Alabama. I stayed with a friend I had gone to college with. I was so afraid that my own son would kill me that I began thinking about selling my home and moving back to Alabama permanently.

That fear did not come from Thoris.

He has never put his hands on me. He has never threatened me. He promised me he would never hurt a single hair on my head—or anyone else for that matter.

But fear does not require facts. It feeds on imagination.

People told me to take out a restraining order so he could not come near my home. These were individuals I called friends. They spoke with such certainty that I began to question my own judgment.

I changed my ADT alarm code. I did not allow my son to come into my home. I built walls where there had once been prayer.

When I took Thoris to court, I believed I was protecting myself. But I was operating from fear, not truth. The judge ruled in Thoris's favor.

Initially, I was very upset. I was convinced he had taken money from me. I believed something was not right.

But my son came to court fully prepared. He brought documentation. He brought receipts. He brought proof showing how the funds were used on my behalf—to make accessibility upgrades in my home so I could safely return after rehab.

He even presented the Facebook post where I publicly thanked God for keeping him alive through his suicide attempts so he could be there for me during my recovery and help prepare my home for my discharge.

In that courtroom, truth confronted fear.

Later, I learned that if the judge had ruled in my favor, it would have reflected permanently on my son's record and could have negatively impacted his ability to secure employment. That realization humbled me. Because a mother should never take bread out of her own child's mouth. I remember speaking to one of the elders at my church about how terrified I was of Thoris. He looked at me and said, "You are not afraid of anything. The way you walk into our treasurer meetings . . . running things—you are not afraid of the elders."

Then God whispered to my heart, "You are not afraid of your son." That whisper broke something inside of me. I realized the fear I was feeling was not rooted in who Thoris truly is. It was rooted in trauma. In outside voices. In my own physical vulnerability after surgery.

My sister, Marilyn Burt Mason, was instrumental in my healing during this season. She reassured me again and again, "Thoris is not going to hurt you." She helped calm my mind. She reminded me of the son I raised.

When Thoris was married and during his previous mental episodes, I would go stay at his home. We would pray together. We would play games. We would watch television. I would stay there so his wife could get some rest. I made sure he took his medication on time.

I was not afraid then. I was a mother covering her child. With prayer and with the love of his mother, he improved every day. So how did I go from staying in his house to running from my own?

Fear.

Fear almost made me lose my son. Fear almost damaged his future. Fear almost fractured what prayer had built.

But God.

God exposed the lie. God corrected my thinking. God restored clarity to my mind.

I had to repent—not publicly, but in my heart—for allowing fear to override love.

Today, I can say with confidence my son is not a threat to me. He is a testimony. Mental illness does not automatically mean violence. Struggle does not mean danger. Healing requires support, not suspicion.

Thank you, Jesus.

Look at God.

He kept my son.

He kept me.

And He kept our relationship from being destroyed by fear.

WHAT THIS MEANS FOR YOUR LIFE

This chapter is a warning to every parent, every friend, and every church member who has someone in their life with mental illness.

Fear is not discernment. Fear looks like discernment. It sounds like wisdom. It masquerades as protection. But 2 Timothy 1:7 says God has not given us a spirit of fear—He has given us power, love, and a sound mind.

I took Thoris to court because people I trusted told me he was dangerous. They told me that people with mental illness kill their families. They told me to protect myself.

None of that was true about him.

But fear does not require facts. It feeds on imagination.

If someone in your life has a mental health diagnosis, do not let other people's fear become your truth. Educate yourself. Talk to their treatment team. Learn the difference between symptoms and threats. And most importantly, ask the person directly—with love, not suspicion—how they are doing.

Mental illness does not automatically mean violence. The vast majority of people with mental illness are more likely to be victims of violence than perpetrators of it. This is not opinion. This is data.

Do not let stigma steal your relationship with someone God has placed in your life.

APPLY THIS

- If you have feared a loved one because of their mental health diagnosis, educate yourself on the actual data about mental illness and violence. Knowledge dissolves fear.
- Evaluate the voices in your ear. Are the people advising you speaking from experience and education—or from fear and assumption?
- If you have damaged a relationship because of fear, consider reaching out with honesty and humility. Reconciliation begins with one truthful conversation.

IF YOU'RE IN A GROUP

- Carolyn admits she was influenced by people who spoke fear into her heart. How do you evaluate the advice you receive from others?
- What is the difference between legitimate concern for safety and stigma-driven fear?
- How can the church better educate its members about mental health to prevent fear from destroying families?

Prayer: Father God, forgive me for allowing fear to speak louder than faith. Thank you for protecting my son's future. Thank you for restoring my clarity of mind. Strengthen every parent battling fear for their child's safety. Replace fear with love and paranoia with peace. In Jesus's name. Amen.

"Fear almost separated us—but prayer brought us back together."

CHAPTER 25

RECONCILIATION ON THE HILL

Written by Thoris Lamar Burt

"Blessed are the peacemakers, for they will be called children of God."

MATTHEW 5:9 (NIV)

There's something about going home that hits different when you've been through hell with the people you love.

In July 2025, my mama and I flew back to Huntsville, Alabama, for the Fourth of July. It wasn't just a trip—it was a quiet kind of healing. The kind that sneaks up on you when God is ready to turn the page.

One afternoon, we drove up to Alabama A&M University—The Hill. Mama worked there for years, studied there, sacrificed there. And I practically grew up in that police department office where she worked.

We drove toward where the police office used to be. Mama couldn't remember the exact location, but for me, it was crystal clear—permanently etched in my childhood. I pointed out where the back entrance once stood, where Butch, the bulldog, and I spent afternoons together.

Sitting there with her, remembering innocence . . . something softened in both of us.

Because the truth is a year earlier, we weren't standing anywhere together.

Back in August 2024, my mama took me to court and had an injunction placed on me—a restraining order. No calling. No texting. No coming within 500 feet.

She accused me of exploiting a vulnerable adult. She said I kept calling and breathing into the phone. She believed I was on drugs. She believed I stole thousands of dollars. She believed I only wanted what I could get from her and my daddy. She believed I would harm her based on things people told her about my mental illness.

But that's not what happened.

On May 8, 2024, I was in a mental fog—deep, disorienting, and terrifying. When she asked for her phone because she couldn't reach it, I panicked and said, "Mama, please don't use it right now." I didn't understand why she burst into tears.

A nurse escorted my mama out. Then the first set of officers arrived—CIT-trained mental health officers, thanks to my brother Terrell. They reassured me: "You're not in any trouble." They treated me with compassion and understanding.

After they left, I still didn't know where my mama was. Time felt distorted. The TV blurred into hallucinations—I remember seeing something like 9/11 happening all over the world.

Then a second set of officers entered—not CIT-trained. The female officer was rude and immediately hostile. She told me I had to leave because I was trespassing.

I tried explaining, "I've been living here 24/7 with a bed the facility provided me to care for my mama." They didn't care. They told me to leave immediately or be arrested.

Growing up around officers at Alabama A&M, I was taught to comply. So, I complied.

But what still haunts me is this: They allowed me—in the middle of a severe mental episode—to drive myself home. I don't remember that drive. Not one mile. Only the grace of God brought me home.

Before leaving, I signed a trespassing warning, though I barely understood it through the fog.

The difference between CIT officers and untrained officers can be the difference between life and death.

And yet... in July 2025, here we were—standing together on The Hill, the place our story began.

Mama talked. I listened.

I talked. She listened.

For the first time in a long time, we weren't talking around the pain—we were talking through it.

On that hill, God stitched us back together. Not instantly. Not perfectly. But faithfully.

Reconciliation isn't loud: it comes in stillness, honesty, shared memory.

Peace was planted that day. And like everything planted on a hill—it will grow.

WHAT THIS MEANS FOR YOUR LIFE

Reconciliation is not a single conversation. It is a season. And it requires three things that most people are unwilling to give: time, honesty, and humility.

My mama and I stood on that hill at Alabama A&M—the place our story began—and talked through pain that was years old. It wasn't dramatic. It wasn't loud. It was two people choosing to face each other instead of away from each other.

If there is a broken relationship in your life that you've been avoiding, I want to give you three steps toward reconciliation:

Step 1: Go back to the beginning. Not to relive the pain, but to remember the love that existed before the fracture. What was beautiful before it broke? Start the conversation there.

Step 2: Listen before you explain. The greatest gift you can give someone in reconciliation is the gift of being heard. Let them speak their full truth before you speak yours.

Step 3: Forgive before you feel ready. Forgiveness is not a feeling; it is a decision. You may not feel reconciled yet. Do it anyway. The feeling follows the faith.

APPLY THIS

- Identify one broken relationship in your life that God is nudging you to reconcile. Write their name down. Pray over it for one week before reaching out.
- When you do reach out, lead with listening. Do not defend. Do not explain. Just hear them.
- If full reconciliation isn't possible, pursue peace. Romans 12:18 says, "If it is possible, as far as it depends on you, live at peace with everyone." Do your part. Release theirs to God.

IF YOU'RE IN A GROUP

- Is there a relationship in your life that needs reconciliation? What's holding you back?
- Thoris and Carolyn reconciled at the same place where their story began. Why do you think going back to the beginning matters?
- What is the difference between reconciliation and pretending nothing happened?

Prayer: Father God, where relationships have been broken by misunderstanding, fear, or pride, mend what only You can mend. Give me the humility to listen before I explain, the courage to forgive before I feel ready, and the patience to walk reconciliation out, one conversation at a time. Where full reconciliation isn't possible, give me peace. And in every fractured place, let Your healing flow. In Jesus's name. Amen.

"Healing doesn't erase the past—it redeems it."

CHAPTER 26

AUGUST 7, 2025–THE LAST STORM

Written by Thoris Lamar Burt

"For he will command his angels concerning you to guard you in all your ways; they will lift you up in their hands, so that you will not strike your foot against a stone."

PSALM 91:11-12 (NIV)

The week of August 7, 2025, God was already preparing me. I just didn't know it yet.

I was deep in a Bible study on John 19:25–27 and John 20:30. John 19 is the moment where Jesus, dying on the cross, looks down and sees His mother—and entrusts her to the disciple John. "Woman, here is your son." John 20:30 reminds the reader that Jesus performed many other signs that were not recorded in the book. Discernment. What to share. What to keep silent on. What was sacred enough to be remembered, and what was not meant for every audience.

I was sitting with those verses for days. I didn't know I was studying my own life.

That same week, an old friend I hadn't spoken to in years reached out after seeing my Facebook post from July 25, 2025—the one where I publicly named, for the first time, the 4 suicide attempts, the loss of my six-figure job, the church that turned me away, and the silence I had been carrying since 2023. The post had cracked something open. And right on cue, this old friend from my teenage church days reappeared in my inbox.

She was a therapist now.

She told me to do something I had never done before. Write down my deepest darkest secrets on a piece of paper. Crumple it up. Put it in the recycle bin. Let it leave the house with the rest of what gets discarded.

So, I did.

I wrote the truths I had never said out loud to anybody other than my therapist and God. I crumpled the paper. I dropped it in the recycle bin. I rolled the bin out to the curb and turned it sideways—not the way you do for normal pickup, but at an angle, like a marker. A signal. *This is a special release. God, take this.*

A few hours later, the recycle bin was empty.

It wasn't recycling day. I know it wasn't recycling day. Or at least I thought I knew. To this day, I cannot tell you with certainty whether what happened that afternoon was God orchestrating a literal release through an unscheduled pickup, or whether I was already starting to hallucinate. I will not pretend to know which one was true. I will only tell you that the secrets that left my body that week never came back to live in it the same way again. The trash man—if there was one—was an angel. Or I was already inside the beginning of the storm. Both can be true.

What I know for sure is that my mind was starting to slip.

I went to the pool one morning that week for sunlight and exercise. Two things every doctor and therapist tells you to do for mental health stability. I sat down, looked up, and saw the eyes of other people glowing and flashing at me. I felt them trying to take over my thoughts. I turned my head away. I tried not to make eye contact. I left the pool and walked home.

That night, lying in bed, I heard something on my roof. Footsteps where there should not be footsteps. Then a vision appeared in my mind, clear as memory: a man dressed in all black, standing on my roof, attempting to infuse poison into my HVAC system. To kill me.

I looked at my phone. A picture of my Orlando Magic mask appeared on the screen.

Out of nowhere.

I got out of bed and went straight to my master bedroom closet because I knew exactly where the mask was. A few weeks earlier, Lorna—the woman who comes to clean my home after my mental episodes—had decluttered that very closet. She had found the mask, held it up to me, and said, "Wash this. You should wash this as soon as possible." I had not yet washed it. But in my mind that night, the picture on my phone was Lorna's voice coming back to me as a sign. *Protect yourself.*

I put the mask on. I got back into bed. I watched smoke begin to come through the vents in my home. I tasted something bitter on my tongue, like metal mixed with chemicals. But the mask was working. The mask was protecting me. The mask was the answer.

I fell asleep with it on.

When I woke up, it was still dark outside, and the voices were already speaking.

Drive out to the Space Coast. There is a spaceship waiting on you. It will take you into outer space, closer to God, where He will heal you from your mental illness.

The voices were calm. They were certain. They were specific. And I obeyed them like a man obeying his pastor.

I got into my car wearing the mask, disoriented, and I pulled out of my driveway.

I did not drive far at first. I went across the street into the neighborhood directly opposite mine and pulled into the empty driveway of a house. I do not know if anyone was home. I do not know what I was waiting for. But I sat there until a Toyota Corolla pulled up in front of the house, turned on its hazard lights, and idled.

My mind made a connection. I drive a Lexus ES350. Lexus is made by Toyota. The Corolla had turned on its hazards. The Corolla was a sign. The Corolla was leading me to the space coast where Toyota—Japanese engineering—would meet rocket engineering—Cape Canaveral—and the spaceship would be waiting for me.

I followed the Corolla. Then I lost it. Then I kept driving anyway, because by then the voices were navigating.

At one point, I pulled into a parking lot, rolled down my window, and asked a security guard if it was possible for me to drive with my head down. Because if I looked up, something bad was going to happen.

He looked at me with a strange look on his face. Then he said, "No, that's not possible. And this is private property. Please leave."

So, I did.

I typed *Kennedy Space Center* into my GPS—because somewhere in the back of my mind, I knew that's where my friend Darryl Gichia-Broussard had worked for years as an engineer for NASA. Then I started thinking about Marshall Space Flight Center, where Jeremy's mother, Marie Malone, had worked at NASA for years. My mind was mixing up coastlines and states and family members, but every wrong turn still pointed at someone who loved me.

I stopped at a convenience store and asked a man in an eighteen-wheeler where Kennedy Space Center was. He pointed me down the road. I drove. I saw the Kennedy Welcome Center, but never the actual center. So, I kept driving. And driving. Until eventually I came to a guarded entry gate with a sign on it.

Blue Origin.

That's when reality hit me.

My brother Jeremy works for Blue Origin. In Huntsville, Alabama. Not Florida. Why was I at Blue Origin's gate in Cape Canaveral wearing an Orlando Magic mask in the middle of the night?

I sat in the car, and I cried.

Not loud crying. Not the kind that shakes you. The kind of crying that arrives when reality returns to a body that has been on a journey it should not have been on. I sat there for about five minutes, and I let myself feel the weight of where I was. Wearing a mask. So many miles from home. Having driven through a hallucination across county lines in my own state.

And then—even through the fog still lifting off my brain—I felt it. *God was keeping me.* He was keeping me even in the middle of the storm. He had used the three space center connections in my actual life—Darryl at Kennedy, Marie at Marshall, Jeremy at Blue Origin—like a three-strand cord pulling me back to reality. He didn't take me to space to heal me. He had already wrapped space around my life through the people who already loved me.

Ecclesiastes 4:12 says a cord of three strands is not quickly broken. I felt that cord at Blue Origin's gate.

I started the engine, and I turned the car around and I began the drive home.

It was somewhere around 3 or 4 o'clock in the morning on August 8, 2025. I was on State Road 528—the Beachline Expressway—heading west out of Cape Canaveral. I had not slept. My body was depleted in a way I cannot describe to anyone who has not been hollowed out by their own brain.

The traffic was heavier than it should have been at that hour. Shift change at Blue Origin. Workers leaving the gates. And mixed in with the cars, eighteen-wheelers. Lots of them. Big rigs hauling freight through the Florida night.

I wanted to pull over and sleep. My body was begging for it. But every time I looked at the shoulder of the road, all I could see was an eighteen-wheeler veering off and crushing my car while I slept inside it. So, I kept driving.

I looked up at the moon, and the devil was in it. His face was in the moon, watching me, smiling, knowing I was tired and trying to kill me before I could get home. My driver's seat began to heat up. The button was off. The indicator light was dark. The heat was on anyway. I pressed the button over and over. The seat kept getting hotter. *The devil is in your car. He is sitting under you. He is heating you up so you will burn.* I started smelling burning oil from the engine. I thought the engine was about to catch fire. The engine was going to explode on the highway, and I was going to die in flames before I could make it home.

But I kept driving.

I kept driving because somewhere deeper than the hallucinations, I knew. **God did not bring me back from Blue Origin's gate to let me die on the Beachline.**

The lane departure assist kept beeping. Every time my eyes closed, every time the car drifted, every time the white line crossed under my tires when it should not have, the car beeped at me. Loud. Insistent. *Wake up. Stay in your lane. Wake up. Stay in your lane.*

Psalm 91:11 says He will command His angels concerning you, to guard you in all your ways. I did not know it that night, but I had angels in beeping sensors. I had cherubim in cruise-control software. I had a guardian engineered into the steering column of a Lexus by people who had never met me, but whose work would keep me alive at four in the morning on the Beachline.

I made it home.

I pulled into my garage.

And then my mind went back to November 26, 2023.

That morning I had been on the floor of this same garage. Not in the car. On the concrete. Lying on my back underneath the tailpipe with a Goodwill bag tucked under my head as a pillow. The car was running. I had been inhaling fumes for over an hour. My phone was vibrating on my chest because Conquistador was calling me—over and over—and I was choosing not to answer because I just wanted to rest. I just wanted it to end.

Now, on August 8, 2025, I was sitting inside the same garage in the same car, and my brain was telling me, *The fumes that did not finish you on November 26 will finish you now.*

I do not know how long I sat in that car. It might have been ten minutes. It might have been thirty. I sat there negotiating with a memory while the storm in my head began to settle.

And then I got out.

By myself. No phone call. No interruption. No friend on the other end refusing to let me go. Just me, opening the door, swinging my legs around, and walking into my house. **The garage that almost killed me on November 26, 2023, was the garage I walked out of on August 8, 2025.**

That is the difference between November 26, 2023 and August 8, 2025. The first time, God sent Conquistador's phone call to pull me out. The second time, He had built enough of me back that I could walk out on my own.

I laid down to sleep, but the paranoia had not fully left me. Before I slept, I went and got aluminum foil from the kitchen, and I went out to my car, and I covered the license plates with foil. Because I was sure that whoever was after me was tracking my plates. The hallucinations had ended. The fear had not.

I want you to know that detail. Because mental illness does not end at the front door. The senses come back before the certainty does.

Later that afternoon, the movers showed up. August 8, 2025, was the day Lorna had arranged for me to pay for and receive the secondhand furniture from the family in Orlando who was moving to Canada—the furniture that would later fill the empty rooms of my home. The same Lorna whose voice in my head had told me to grab the Orlando Magic mask the month before. The mask had covered me through the night. The furniture would fill my house in the late afternoon.

She did not know what God had used her for. Neither did I until I sat down to write this chapter.

After the movers left, I picked up the phone, and I called Mama. I called my father, Thomas. I called my Godfather, Johnny. I called my brother Jeremy. I called my friend Darryl. The link to the three space center cords that had pulled me back at the gate were now back on the phone, witnessing what I had just survived. I did not admit myself to the hospital this time. Because for the first time in my history of episodes, I was fully aware of what had happened. I knew it was the storm. I knew God had kept me through it. And I knew the storm had passed.

That same month, I began the conversation with my psychiatrist, Maurice Foster, that would change everything. In November 2025, Maurice suggested I complete the Myriad genetic test—a pharmacogenetic test that analyzes how your specific genes respond to different psychiatric medications. The test identifies which medications are most likely to work for your unique biology and which ones are likely to do nothing or do harm.

When the results came back, the medication I had been prescribed in August 2025—right after the Blue Origin night—was identified as the *A range preferred medication* for my body. Out of every option, the one God had already put in my mouth was the one my DNA had been waiting for.

It is now May 2026. I am writing this chapter on the anniversary of the May 4, 2025 crisis that came before this one. I have been episode-free since August 7, 2025. **And I claim in the name of Jesus that I will be episode-free as of August 7, 2026, and beyond.**

August 7, 2025, was the last storm.

He kept me through every one. But this one—He told me to look back and tell the world about. So, the next person whose senses turn on them will know they are not alone. And the next person whose car beeps them awake will know an angel is on the road with them. And the next person sitting in the garage where they almost died will know they can still get out and walk inside.

WHAT THIS MEANS FOR YOUR LIFE

There is a particular kind of fear that visits people who live with mental illness: the fear that one day your own brain will turn on you so completely that you will not be able to find your way back. That you will be lost inside your own head, and nobody will be able to reach you.

I want to tell you what August 7, 2025, taught me, so you can carry it into the storms you have not yet survived.

Lesson 1: Your five senses can lie to you. God doesn't need them to keep you. That night, my eyes saw the devil in the moon. My ears heard voices ordering me to drive to a spaceship. My skin felt heat where there was no heat. My nose smelled fire where there was no fire. My tongue tasted poison where there was no poison. Every single sense I had ever trusted to tell me what was real was lying to me at the same time. And yet, the Keeper kept me. He used a beeping sensor in a car I had bought years before I needed it. He used three people in my life who happened to work in or near the space industry. I had a phone call from with an old friend I hadn't spoken with in years who just so happened to be a therapist. He used a cleaning lady's offhand comment about a mask. God does not require your faculties to be functional to keep you. He works around the broken ones. This is the heart of why HE kept me on August 7, 2025. And it is the reason HE can keep you when your own mind betrays you.

Lesson 2: Pre-positioned grace is a real thing. Look for yours. Before the storm came, God had already arranged safety nets. Lorna had already found the mask. The Bible study had already given me verses about discernment. The therapist friend had already shown up in my inbox. Three people I loved already worked at 3 different space facilities. The car I drove already had lane departure assist built into it. None of that was last-minute. God was placing protection long before I needed it. He has done the same for you. Look around your life right now. Who has been placed in your path? What tools have you been given that you didn't even know you would need? Stop and thank God for the safety nets you have not yet fallen into. They are not coincidences. They are preparation.

Lesson 3: Some storms end without a hospital. That's not a failure of severity; that's a marker of growth. I did not admit myself this time. Not because the episode was less serious, but because it was the most serious one I had ever survived. But because the same man who had been hospitalized in 2018, attempted suicide in 2023, and called the police on himself in 2025 had now grown enough that he could walk through the storm and come out the other side recognizing it. Growth in mental health management does not always mean fewer storms. Sometimes it means greater awareness inside the storm. I want you to give yourself credit for the awareness you have built. If you can now name what is happening inside you while it is happening, you have already grown more than you realize.

Lesson 4: Get the pharmacogenetic test. If you are struggling with psychiatric medication—or you are on your 3rd or 4th medication trial—ask your psychiatrist about pharmacogenetic testing. The one I took is GeneSight, the pharmacogenomic test from Myriad Genetics. It is a cheek swab. The results identify which medications are most likely to work with your specific biology. Most people who live with serious mental illness have never been told this test exists. I was nearly fifty years old before anyone mentioned it to me. I do not want that to be your story. The right medication can change the trajectory of your life. The right medication is part of how God keeps you.

Lesson 5: Claim your last storm forward. You may not yet have had your last storm. You may not even believe a last storm is possible. I understand. But hear me: The act of speaking your healing into being is part of how it becomes real. I am writing this from May 2026, having been episode-free for 9 months. I do not know what August 2026 holds, but I am claiming it in Jesus's name. And I am writing it in this book so that when the next anniversary comes, there will be a record of what I believed before I knew. Faith is the substance of things hoped for, the evidence of things not seen (Hebrews 11:1). Speak your last storm forward. Then live like you believe it.

APPLY THIS

- Make an appointment with your psychiatrist this week and ask about pharmacogenetic testing. Specifically mention Myriad or GeneSight. If your psychiatrist is unfamiliar, ask for a referral who is. This is the single most actionable step in this entire book.
- Identify your three-strand cord. Write down three people in your life right now who could pull you back to reality if your mind ever lost it. Tell them they are on your list. Make sure they know what to do if you call.

- Write down your "last storm." Even if it has not happened yet, claim it in faith. Date it. Speak it. Put it somewhere you will see it again.

IF YOU'RE IN A GROUP

- Have you ever experienced your senses lying to you? In a smaller way, like a panic attack or a moment of disorientation? What did it teach you about what is "real"?
- Thoris describes three space-center connections that pulled him back to reality. Who are the people God has pre-positioned in your life that could be your three-strand cord during a crisis?
- What does it mean to claim a "last storm" while still living in the possibility of more storms? Is that faith, denial, or both?

Prayer: Father God, thank you for being the Keeper my five senses could not be. Thank you for placing angels in beeping sensors, in cleaning ladies' offhand comments, in old friends' unexpected phone calls, and in family members who happen to work in the industries my mind would later try to escape into. Thank you for the medication You ordained for my body. Thank you for the doctors and the test and the Spirit-led decisions that brought the right pill to the right mouth at the right time. Thank you that August 7, 2025, was the last storm. And in faith, I declare that August 7, 2026, will mark a full year of continued keeping. For anyone reading this in the middle of their own storm, let them feel Your hand right now. Let them remember the three people You have placed in their life. Let them know that even when their mind cannot tell what is real, You are real, and You are keeping them. In Jesus's might, matchless, miracle-working name. Amen.

"When all five senses lied,

He still told the truth."

PART VII

RESTING: THE PURPOSE BEHIND THE PAIN (2025-2026)

Core Teaching: Rest is not retreat—it is resurrection.

CHAPTER 27

YOU CAN'T POUR FROM AN EMPTY CUP–CLEARING MY MIND

Written by Thoris Lamar Burt

"I am the vine; you are the branches. If you remain in me and I in you, you will bear much fruit; apart from me you can do nothing."

JOHN 15:5 (NIV)

If you're drained mentally, emotionally, physically, or financially, you simply cannot be the best version of yourself—not for others, and not even for you. You can try to push through, you can try to force momentum, you can try to act strong… but the truth is simple: an empty cup can't pour anything.

On August 20, 2025, my Auntie—Marilyn Burt-Mason, whom I lovingly call Murt—spoke a word into my life. That day, I shared pictures of some secondhand furniture I'd recently bought for my home. To me, it was more than furniture; it was a blessing.

After my divorce, my home felt hollow—physically and emotionally. There were empty rooms, empty corners, empty spaces I didn't have the money to fill. No matter how much I longed for comfort or coziness or a sense of belonging, my budget said, "Not right now."

But God's timing is undefeated. When He arranges a blessing, it fits.

I stumbled across furniture priced so perfectly that it could only have been God's doing—pieces that didn't just fill my home but filled my spirit with gratitude.

I'd never shared pictures of my home with Murt until that day. I sent exterior shots, interior shots, and the furniture that I knew God Himself had ordained for me to find. And her response stopped me in my tracks—because she didn't just see furniture . . . she saw me.

She said, "Your home is beautiful! The furniture is absolutely gorgeous, and, yes, God has sho'nuff blessed you. I think this will help you heal along with your upcoming baptism. God is making your life complete. You had empty space in your home and empty space in your heart."

Her words hit me because they were true.

My home had felt dark, quiet, and heavy in a way I couldn't fully articulate. Even my best friend, Mario Ballantyne, felt it when he visited after my divorce. He gently told me that the emptiness in my house mirrored the emptiness in my spirit.

And he was right.

What Murt helped me see is that God doesn't just fill rooms—He restores souls. He doesn't just supply furniture—He supplies healing. He doesn't just complete homes—He completes hearts.

The empty spaces I lived with weren't just physical. They were emotional. Spiritual. Grief-shaped. Divorce-shaped. Healing-shaped.

And little by little . . . blessing by blessing . . . prayer by prayer . . . God began filling both.

Because you can't pour from an empty cup—but you also can't stay empty when God Himself is pouring into you.

There comes a moment in every journey where the battlefield shifts from the outside world to the inside of your own mind. For years, I fought people, circumstances, expectations, deadlines, disappointments, and disruptions. But one day, God made it clear: The real battle was in my mind, and the real victory would be too.

Romans 12:2 says "Do not conform to the pattern of this world, but be transformed by the renewing of your *mind. Then you will be able to test and approve what God's will is—his good, pleasing* ***and perfect will.***"— This isn't just a scripture you memorize. It's a scripture you survive.

The world told me: Be strong. Hide your pain. Push through the trauma. Pretend your mind doesn't scare you sometimes.

But God said: Be transformed. Renew your mind. Lay down the patterns you inherited, the patterns you adopted, the patterns that almost killed you.

This chapter is that transformation. This chapter is the renewing. This chapter is the clearing.

Before I ever stepped into therapy, before the diagnoses, before the medications, before SSDI, before Room 235, before the suicide attempt on November 26, 2023 . . . my mind was overcrowded.

Crowded with fear. Crowded with shame. Crowded with years of "be strong" even when strong was killing me.

I carried the weight of being the responsible one. The dependable one. The "he'll figure it out" one. The "he's always okay" one.

But I wasn't okay. Not even close.

And the scariest battles?

They weren't loud. They were silent. They were mental. They were spiritual.

Romans 12:2 told me transformation begins with the renewing of the mind—but you can't renew what you won't acknowledge is damaged.

I had to acknowledge it.

God was saying, "You've worked long enough on the outside. Now it's time to work on your mind."

Rest wasn't a reward. Rest wasn't a retirement. Rest wasn't a setback.

Rest was treatment. Rest was therapy. Rest was renewal.

Therapy wasn't about getting advice. Therapy was about clearing debris—mental rubble I didn't even know existed.

There, I learned that I wasn't broken—I was overloaded. I wasn't weak—I was wounded. I wasn't crazy—I was carrying trauma too heavy for one person. I wasn't dramatic—I was surviving.

Therapy taught me how to regulate my emotions, understand my triggers, recognize mental spirals, rebuild thought patterns, and breathe again—mentally and spiritually.

Clearing my mind meant unlearning who trauma told me I was and relearning who God always knew I was.

Transformation is an ongoing, continuous, daily activity.

Renewing the mind is a journey, not a destination.

For me, that renewing looks like forgiving myself, resting without guilt, celebrating survival, choosing peace over panic, choosing therapy over silence, choosing honesty over image, choosing God over expectations.

And most importantly, choosing life.

Every day.

On purpose.

Clearing my mind didn't mean erasing my past. It meant understanding it. It meant owning it. It meant healing from it.

Now, when I look in the mirror, I don't see the man who almost let go. I see the man God held onto.

I don't see the fog. I see the clarity.

I don't see the crisis. I see the calling.

Renewing my mind has become my lifestyle—my discipline—my worship.

And this chapter of my life, this clarity, this transformation?

This is why He kept me.

WHAT THIS MEANS FOR YOUR LIFE

Before I could heal my life, I had to clear my mind. Before I could clear my mind, I had to acknowledge it was crowded. And before I could acknowledge it was crowded, I had to stop pretending I was fine.

Romans 12:2 says, "Be transformed by the renewing of your mind." That word "renewing" is active and continuous. It is not a one-time event; it is a daily discipline.

Here is what renewing your mind looks like in practice:

Daily Practice 1: Identify the thought before it becomes a belief. Not every thought that enters your mind belongs there. Learn to evaluate: Is this thought from God, from trauma, or from fear? If it doesn't align with God's Word, it doesn't deserve residence in your mind.

Daily Practice 2: Replace the lie with truth. When depression says, "You're a burden," replace it with Psalm 139:14—"I am fearfully and wonderfully made." When anxiety says, "Something terrible is about to happen," replace it with Jeremiah 29:11—"plans to give you hope and a future." Replacement is not denial. It is warfare.

Daily Practice 3: Fill the empty spaces intentionally. My home had empty rooms. My heart had empty spaces. God filled both—but I had to let Him. Sometimes healing means making room for new things by releasing the grief over what's gone.

Daily Practice 4: Rest without guilt. Rest is not laziness. Rest is obedience. Jesus rested. God Himself rested on the seventh day. If the Creator of the universe took a break, you are allowed to take one too.

APPLY THIS

- Identify one recurring negative thought you have about yourself. Write it down. Then write the biblical truth that contradicts it. Read both out loud.
- Identify one "empty space" in your life—emotional, relational, or physical—that you've been avoiding. Ask God what He wants to put there.
- Schedule one hour this week that is dedicated to rest. Not productivity disguised as rest. Actual rest.

IF YOU'RE IN A GROUP

- What does "renewing your mind" look like practically in your daily life?
- Thoris says God doesn't just fill rooms—He restores souls. What empty space in your life is God currently filling?
- Why is rest so difficult for many people—especially people of faith? How do we change that?

Prayer: Father God, renew my mind. Where lies have taken up residence, evict them with Your truth. Where exhaustion has crowded out joy, restore me. Teach me to rest without guilt, to fill empty spaces with what You've chosen, and to abide in You as a daily practice rather than a destination. Be both the vine and the gardener of my life. In Jesus's name. Amen.

"When God starts filling your empty places, even the broken pieces begin to make sense. Healing begins when the mind stops running and finally sits still long enough for God to speak."

CHAPTER 28

PROVING I WAS BROKEN ENOUGH—RETIREMENT AT 47

When God Says, "Rest"

Written by Thoris Lamar Burt

"The righteous person may have many troubles, but the Lord delivers him from them all."

PSALM 34:19 (NIV)

There are dates that carve themselves into your spirit.

Birthdays. Funerals. Divorce decrees.

And then there are the dates you survive by nothing but mercy.

For me, that date is November 26, 2023.

The day I tried to die for the fourth time.

The day everything broke open.

The day SSA would later mark as my official SSDI onset date.

But before the garage … before the fumes … before the phone kept ringing …

There was a storm eroding me from the inside.

Mental illness doesn't announce itself. It doesn't say, "Today I'm taking everything." It slips in quietly—through insomnia, mania, depression, hallucinations, paranoia, racing thoughts, fear, shame.

For months, I wasn't myself. My mind was moving too fast and too slow at the same time. Mania had me wired. Depression had me drowning. I wasn't sleeping. I wasn't eating. I wasn't functioning.

I was unraveling in silence—the kind of silence people call *strength* because they can't hear your soul screaming.

And then I hit a breaking point, and I made four attempts to end my life.

They weren't cries for attention.

They weren't dramatics.

They were a man whose illness had turned inward and lethal.

- The first attempt—impulsive despair.
- The second—darkness with planning.
- The third—methodical and almost final.
- The fourth—November 26, 2023.

My car.

My garage.

The engine running.

The door closed.

Over an hour of fumes filling the air. I know I should have been dead, but God saved me.

I laid on my back under the tailpipe, using a Goodwill donation bag as a pillow.

"I just want to rest."

That's what I told myself.

That day became my SSDI onset date.

Because no one survives their breaking point unchanged.

And I was changed. I was broken. I'd walked out of that garage barely breathing. Changed.

I would not have applied for SSDI a year earlier. I would not have been able to overcome the shame of it. I didn't announce I was applying for SSDI. I didn't post about it. I didn't say it out loud in rooms where productivity equals worth.

Mental illness invites suspicion the moment you name it.

If you don't limp, people assume you can walk. If you don't bleed, they assume you're fine.

That was the first shame.

Before the system doubted me, I doubted myself.

I had worked for decades. Led teams. Carried responsibility.

So, applying didn't feel like relief. It felt like surrender. The forms didn't ask how hard I tried. They asked how broken I was. How often do symptoms occur? How long do they last? What can you no longer do?

It wasn't paperwork. It was a cross-examination. Honesty wasn't enough. If I minimized anything—the way I'd been trained to do professionally—I wouldn't be believed. I had to magnify my worst days. I had to convince strangers my mind was dangerous to me. That kind of exposure strips your dignity.

Work didn't end; it collapsed.

At Deltek, I knew managing people was too heavy. Not because I lacked skill. Because my mind couldn't carry it anymore.

I asked to transition into an individual contributor role. HR gave me sixty days. Sixty days to apply. Sixty days to interview. Sixty days to save my job. I followed the process. Then the hiring freeze hit. The roles vanished. The clock didn't.

In mental fog, I signed a document stating that if no internal role was secured within sixty days, I would resign. No ADA flexibility. No pause. Just policy.

I didn't quit. The system closed in. I tried again at Cogent Communications.

Three days.

That's how long I lasted. Three days before a mental health crisis ended it. By then, SSDI wasn't optional; it was survival.

The problem was that mental health claims don't come easy.

SSA wants proof.

But you can't X-ray schizoaffective disorder. There's no MRI for hallucinations. No blood test for mania. No scan for suicidal ideation. Mental health disability cases are hard because symptoms fluctuate. One day, you look fine. The next day, you can't leave your house.

Proof becomes therapy notes, psychiatric records, crisis interventions, missed work, and the inability to function consistently. And while gathering all that documentation—you're still fighting to stay alive.

The claims were denied. Again, and again.

The letters came in neutral language. Clinical. Detached. Final.

"Not disabled enough."

They didn't say those exact words. But that was the message. All that vulnerability. All that exposure. And still unseen.

I considered quitting the process. Because having to prove your pain repeatedly is its own kind of violence. I pulled back. I stopped explaining. I let silence grow. Shame deepens in isolation.

And then approval came. One day. With no fanfare.

There was no celebration. No victory dance. Just relief.

Like air returning after being underwater too long.

SSDI wasn't a reward. It was acknowledgment. It didn't erase what happened in that garage. It confirmed that what happened mattered.

God didn't shame me. Systems did. But even then, He kept me alive long enough to be believed; that's why this chapter matters. Not because I was approved. But because I endured long enough to reach the day when help finally stopped asking me to prove I was broken and simply let me live.

There are moments in life when God doesn't whisper—He commands. Not in a tone of judgment or force, but in a tone of love so deep that it shakes you free from everything you didn't even realize was wearing you down. That's what Matthew 11:28 felt like the day I received the call confirming my SSDI approval. I didn't just hear the verse ... I felt it.

"Come to me ... and I will give you rest."

Rest. A word I had run from for years. A word I never thought applied to me. But when God says "rest," you don't negotiate—you surrender.

Most people would see getting approved for SSDI at age forty-seven as paperwork, timing, and coincidence. But I've lived long enough, survived long enough, and discerned enough to know when something is bigger than it looks.

And this was bigger.

Because forty-seven isn't just a number. Not for me. Not for my story.

In Huntsville, Alabama—the place where I was born, the soil where my story began—the automobile tag code is forty-seven. Anyone from Huntsville knows that number. It marks you. It lets the world know where you come from before you even say a word.

So, when I got approved at the exact age that matched my hometown tag number, I didn't shrug it off. I knew God was speaking in a language only the Spirit-filled could interpret.

Forty-seven wasn't a coincidence; it was a confirmation. A reminder that my story was coming full circle. God was bringing me back to my roots. The place that birthed me would also be the place symbolic of a rebirth. Rest was not an ending—it was a divine homecoming.

And isn't that just like God? To use a detail so small, so ordinary, so easily overlooked... to make a statement so unmistakably divine.

I often think back to where my work ethic truly began—not in Orlando, not in corporate America, not in sales rooms or boardrooms, but at the NCO Club on Redstone Arsenal in Huntsville, Alabama. I was just fourteen years old, stepping into adulthood earlier than most kids my age. Mama signed the papers so I could get a work permit, believing in me before I even understood what responsibility really meant.

My first job? A dishwasher at the NCO Club. Hot water, steaming trays, clanking silverware. It wasn't glamorous, but it was holy ground—the first place I learned to work with pride, hustle with humility, and carry myself like someone who mattered.

It still blows my mind that the boy who earned his first paycheck on Redstone soil would one day be divinely retired at age forty-seven—the number that represents the very city where my story started.

It was as if God was saying, "Your working years began in Huntsville... and at forty-seven, I'm taking you back to that number to show you your story has come full circle."

And I was ready for that rest.

People didn't know. People saw the strength. People heard the laughter. People watched me show up for my mama, for my family, for work, for life. But what they didn't see was the weight. The pressure. The nights of anxiety turning into mornings of exhaustion. The depression that moved in silently and refused to leave. The May 8th crisis that nearly broke me. The November 26th suicide attempt that could've ended everything.

They didn't see the battles I fought behind closed doors... the battles God watched.

By the time SSDI was approved, I wasn't just tired. I wasn't just drained. I was weary in my bones—the kind of weariness you can't sleep off, can't pray away instantly, can't push through by willpower alone.

God knew. God saw. God intervened.

And He said, "Son, you've carried enough. Now... rest."

When people hear the word "retirement," they imagine Florida beaches, gold watches, decades of corporate loyalty, a celebration with cake and cheap champagne.

But retirement for me didn't come with balloons or applause. It came with silence.

A holy silence. A healing silence. A silence where God finally had room to speak without me trying to outrun His voice.

I didn't retire because life defeated me. I retired because God rescued me.

Let me say that again: I didn't retire because I couldn't keep going. I retired because God said I didn't need to.

Forty-seven became the age where the world expected work, but God expected rest. Forty-seven became the bridge between the boy born in Huntsville, the man who fought battles in Orlando, and the survivor who now walks in purpose.

Forty-seven became the age where I put my hands down long enough for God to place something new in them.

People don't talk enough about the emotional toll of applying for SSDI. The vulnerability. The fear. The feeling of being judged by strangers who know nothing about your pain. You submit your life on paper—every hospital visit, every crisis, every suicide attempt, every mental-health episode, every medication adjustment—and then you wait, which is its own form of suffering. And the denials? They feel like someone telling you your pain isn't real.

But when the approval finally came, something inside me shifted.

I didn't feel ashamed. I didn't feel weak. I didn't feel "less than." I felt seen. I felt heard. I felt carried.

For once in my life, the system didn't break me—it believed me.

And God used that approval to declare something over my life: "You have fought long enough. This season is Mine."

Rest isn't quitting. Rest isn't retreat. Rest isn't resignation.

Rest is recovery. Rest is recalibration. Rest is resurrection. Rest is obedience.

Jesus didn't say, "Come to me, and I'll train you harder."

He said, "Come to me . . . and I will give you rest."

Rest is a gift—one many people refuse because they think rest means weakness. But after everything I've survived, rest feels like strength. It feels like permission to breathe in ways I never allowed myself to before.

Rest has allowed me to reconnect with my mama, rebuild parts of myself therapy didn't reach until recently, reflect on the tragedies that could have ended me, write the book that is helping me heal chapter by chapter, understand my mental health in ways that finally make sense, and stand in my truth without apology.

WHAT THIS MEANS FOR YOUR LIFE

There are two kinds of battles most people never discuss: the battle of proving your pain to strangers and the battle of accepting that rest is holy.

On proving your pain: If you are navigating a disability claim, a medical leave, an ADA accommodation, or any process that requires you to document your suffering for someone else's approval—I want you to know that the shame you feel is not yours to carry. You did not choose illness. You did not choose crisis. You are asking for help that you earned by surviving.

The system is not designed to believe you quickly. It is designed to test your endurance. That is unjust, but it is the reality. Document everything. Save every record. Get professional representation if you can. And do not let denial letters define your worth.

On accepting rest: When God says rest, He means it. Not as punishment. Not as retirement from purpose. But as preparation for the next assignment.

Matthew 11:28 doesn't say, "Come to me all who are weary and I'll give you more work." It says, "I will give you rest." If God Himself is offering it, stop apologizing for receiving it.

Forty-seven wasn't just an age. It was a message—a spiritual callback to where my story began. Huntsville. North Alabama. The 47-license tag. God was saying, "Your working years began in Huntsville at 14... and at 47, I'm returning you to rest."

APPLY THIS

- If you are navigating SSDI, disability, or medical leave: you are not a burden. You are a person accessing a system designed to help you. Let go of the shame.
- If you have been denied, do not give up. Appeals exist for a reason. Get an advocate or attorney if possible.

- If God is calling you to rest and you keep resisting, ask yourself why. Is it pride? Is it identity? Is it fear of what people will think? Name the resistance. Then surrender it.

IF YOU'RE IN A GROUP

- How does society's emphasis on productivity make it difficult for people to accept rest as a gift from God?
- Thoris says, "Having to prove your pain repeatedly is its own kind of violence." How does that resonate with you?
- What would change in our churches if we celebrate seasons of rest the same way we celebrate seasons of hustle?

Prayer: Father God, thank you for delivering me from many troubles—the ones I survived and the ones You spared me from without my knowing. Where I have had to prove my pain, vindicate me. Where the world has called rest weakness, redefine it through Your Word. Help me receive Your invitation to rest as the holy gift it is—preparation, not punishment. Resurrection, not retreat. In Jesus's name, Amen.

"The hardest part wasn't losing my jobs. It was having to prove my pain to people who never lived inside my mind. Sometimes God doesn't close a chapter—He simply makes you lie down, so you can rise again healed."

CHAPTER 29

FINAL WORD: WHY HE KEPT ME

Written by Thoris Lamar Burt

"To him who is able to keep you from stumbling and to present you before his glorious presence without fault and with great joy—to the only God our Savior be glory, majesty, power and authority, through Jesus Christ our Lord, before all ages, now and forevermore! Amen."

JUDE 1:24-25 (NIV)

In the end, when all the pages close, all the chapters settle, and all the memories find their place, one truth rises above every moment in my story: God kept me. Over and over again . . . HE kept me.

This final chapter isn't about survival—it's about revelation. This is the moment I finally understand why He kept me through every storm, every breakdown, every miracle, every moment that should've taken me out but didn't.

This is the chapter where hindsight becomes healing and every piece of my life fits into God's greater pattern—one I didn't always see, but one He was always writing.

Depression had me in ways nobody saw. Anxiety had me in ways nobody understood. To the outside world, I looked functional, capable, strong . . . but inside, I was unraveling piece by piece.

God kept me because He knew the war in my mind wasn't a sign of weakness—it was a sign of warfare. And He refused to let the enemy win a battle I didn't even have the strength to fight alone.

He kept me because there was a future version of me that needed to exist. He kept me because silence is not surrender. He kept me because even when I let go, He didn't.

Sunday, November 26, 2023, God kept me. I survived the garage not because I was strong, but because God wasn't done.

May 8th, 2024. The mental fog at The Mayflower should have ended my story right there. God guided me home through a fog that could've destroyed me.

He kept me because purpose cannot die in confusion. He kept me because healing was waiting in Room 235. He kept me because reconciliation was on the other side of that crisis. He kept me because Mama needed me. And because I needed me—even if I didn't realize it yet.

Room 235 wasn't random. It wasn't luck. It wasn't just a room assignment at a rehab facility. It was divine staging.

Room 235 became holy ground. The paintings were prophecy. The colors were confirmation. The atmosphere was alignment.

When I spoke with my mentor on a Zoom call from that room, he saw it instantly. He said, "This room is full of signs—healing, reconciliation, recovery, return." This was a man who has walked with God long enough to recognize the difference between coincidence and communication. He didn't know anything about the room. I didn't show him the paintings on purpose. I simply turned my camera slightly, and the artwork slipped into the frame behind me.

He leaned in. Paused. And with that calm, steady authority that only comes from spiritual maturity, he said:

"Thoris ... do you see what God is showing you behind you? This room is full of signs."

I froze. "What do you mean?" I asked.

He smiled.

"Those paintings aren't just decorations. They speak healing. They speak reconciliation. They speak recovery. They speak return ..."

Healing. Reconciliation. Recovery. Return.

Exactly the things I prayed for.

My mentor continued, "The blue is peace. The gold is glory. The green is restoration. The movement in the strokes represents God rewriting your story. And the fact that these paintings are behind you while you talk about your journey means God has already gone before you."

God kept me because Room 235 was where my mind began to clear, where my relationship with Mama was restored, where I could finally breathe again after years of holding it together.

He kept me because He needed me to see Him—in art, in color, in timing, in unexpected symbols, in a room designed for healing before I even knew I needed healing.

He kept me because my rest was overdue. He kept me because burnout had become part of my identity. He kept me because He knew I needed permission to stop performing and start healing.

He kept me so He could say, "Your work began in Huntsville at 14 . . . and at 47, I'm returning you to rest."

There were moments I thought my marriage breaking apart meant I was broken. Moments where mental illness was misunderstood, feared, misinterpreted, weaponized without intent.

But even in the heartbreak—even in the misdiagnosed assumptions, the fear, the stigma, the unraveling—God kept me because He knew love lost does not mean purpose lost.

He kept me through the shame. He kept me through the confusion. He kept me through the loneliness. And He restored me in ways no relationship ever could.

Of all the reasons God kept me alive, this one feels the most sacred: He kept me because Mama needed me. He kept me because I needed to be the one to show up for her spinal surgery journey. He kept me because it was time to heal our relationship.

He kept me so Mama could look at me again and say, "I trust you."

He kept me for reconciliation, for restoration, for redemption.

He kept me because other people's breakthroughs are tied to my obedience. He kept me because someone needed this book. He kept me because someone needs the transparency, the honesty, the truth of a man saying, "I almost let go—but God held on."

He kept me to break generational patterns. He kept me to testify. He kept me so my scars could speak louder than silence ever could. He didn't keep me for who I was. He kept me for who I'm becoming.

A man who sees. A man who discerns. A man who heals. A man who rests. A man who loves. A man who walks boldly in truth. A man whose mind is clear. A man whose future is aligned. A man who lived through what should have killed him.

And now... I finally understand.

Why He kept me in the garage, in the fog, in Room 235, in depression, in anxiety, through rejection, through misunderstanding, through spiritual warfare, through near-death moments, through every season that tried to take me out.

He kept me because I am His.

WHAT THIS MEANS FOR YOUR LIFE: THE SEVEN REASONS GOD KEEPS YOU

I survived the garage. I survived the fog. I survived the divorce. I survived the hospitalizations. I survived the accusations. I survived the shame. And I survived long enough to understand why.

Here is what I know now about why God keeps His children, and I believe these reasons apply to you as much as they apply to me:

Reason 1: Because purpose must live. God has a plan for your life that has not yet been completed. Your story is not finished. The fact that you are reading this page is proof.

Reason 2: Because someone needs what you survived. Your testimony is not just your own. It belongs to every person who is fighting the same battle in silence. Your survival gives them permission to survive too.

Reason 3: Because generational cycles must be broken. You may be the person in your family line who stops the cycle of silence, shame, addiction, or despair. That assignment is worth living for.

Reason 4: Because healing is still in progress. God doesn't keep you alive just to leave you wounded. He keeps you alive to heal you, and healing takes time. Give yourself that time.

Reason 5: Because your family needs your presence, not your perfection. Your children don't need a perfect parent. They need a present one. Your mama doesn't need you to be strong. She needs you to be alive.

Reason 6: Because the enemy doesn't get the final word. Every time you wake up, you are a living contradiction of every lie the enemy ever told you. Your existence is warfare. Your breath is rebellion against darkness.

Reason 7: Because God refuses to release what He has claimed. Jude 1:24 says He is able to keep you from stumbling. Not might. Not sometimes. Able. And what God holds, nothing can take.

You are kept. Not because you are perfect. Not because you are strong. Not because you earned it. But because He is faithful.

And that is why HE kept me.

APPLY THIS

- Which of the seven reasons resonated most deeply with you? Write it down and put it where you can see it daily.
- Write your own "Why HE Kept Me" statement in one sentence. Carry it with you.
- Tell someone your testimony this week. Not the polished version. The real one. Someone needs to hear it.

IF YOU'RE IN A GROUP

- Which of the seven reasons hit you the hardest? Why?
- Thoris says, "Your existence is warfare. Your breath is rebellion against darkness." How does that reframe the way you see your daily life?
- If you had to write your own "Why HE Kept Me" statement, what would it say?

Prayer: Father God, thank you for every person who turned these pages. Thank you for every heart that recognized pieces of itself in this testimony. Thank you for every weary soul that whispered, "This is my story too." And thank you for the divine appointment that led them here. Lord, I pray a hedge of protection over each reader—mind, body, and spirit. Where there is anxiety, bring peace. Where there is depression, bring light. Where there is trauma, bring healing. Where there is confusion, bring clarity. Where there is shame, bring freedom. Where there is brokenness, bring restoration. Cover their homes. Cover their families. Cover their minds from attacks seen and unseen. Remind them that You are the Keeper—the same Keeper who held me in my lowest valley and highest breakthrough. If they are fighting silent battles, speak louder than the lies in their heads. If they are tired, give them rest. If they are holding on by a thread, place Your hand beneath theirs. Lord, let this book not just be words—let it be medicine. Let it be confirmation. Let it be deliverance. Let it be the beginning of their healing journeys. And when they doubt... when the night feels long, when the tears feel heavy, when the road feels impossible... remind them: You kept them before. You will keep them again. In the mighty, matchless, miracle-working name of Jesus. Amen.

"I survived because God refused to let go—and now I live to tell why."

AFTERWORD

When I look back over the pages of this book—over the storms, the scars, the signs, the symbols, the miracles—I see something I couldn't see while living through it: I was never walking alone.

Not in the garage. Not in the fog. Not during the suicide attempt. Not during the panic spirals. Not during the sleepless nights or tear-stained mornings. Not during the divorce. Not during the evaluations and appointments. Not during the long stretch of waiting for SSDI. Not even during the moments when my own mind betrayed me.

Every step had His fingerprints. Every chapter had His hand on it. Every breakdown had a breakthrough hiding behind it. Every ending I feared was actually a beginning God was preparing.

Today, I live with a mind that is clearer than it has ever been. A heart more open than it has ever been. A relationship with Mama restored. A purpose rooted in healing and truth. A peace that makes no human sense.

I am not the man who almost let go. I am the man God refused to release.

And the truth is . . . I'm still becoming. Still healing. Still learning myself. Still learning God. Still waking up to new mercy every single morning.

This book ends—but my story doesn't.

If these pages found you in your own storm, my prayer is that you now know you are kept, too.

Kept by grace. Kept by purpose. Kept by a God who stays. Always.

ACKNOWLEDGMENTS

To God—the Keeper of my soul, the Author of every chapter, and the One who refused to release His grip even when I tried to let go. This book exists because You said, "Live." Thank you for mercy that outran my mistakes and grace that carried me through storms I didn't think I'd survive.

To my mother, Carolyn Virginia Burt—the heartbeat of my story. Your resilience shaped me. Your prayers protected me. Your trust restored me. This book is as much your testimony as it is mine. Everything I am, everything I survived, everything I hope to become—it traces back to you.

To my father, Thomas Lee Malone—thank you for the part of me that comes from you. Even through distance and silence, I carried pieces of your identity with me. I honor you for your role in my beginning. Without you, there would be no me—and without me, this testimony would not exist.

To my Godfather, Johnny Alberto Bryant—thank you for being a steady presence, a covering, and a source of quiet strength throughout my life. Your belief in me and your spiritual insight shaped me in ways I'm still discovering.

To my siblings—Terrell, Tracy, Martina, TJ, and Jeremy—each of you holds a piece of my heart and story. Your prayers, forgiveness, devotionals, and even your distance have shaped me. I pray this book becomes a bridge back to love and healing.

To my best friends—Kristy Reyes Blackburn, Mario Ballantyne, Darryl Gichia-Broussard, and Conquistador—thank you for your unwavering presence.

To my Aunties—Marilyn Burt Mason (Murt), Crystal Love—thank you for your wisdom, grounding, and the generational strength you passed down.

To my extended family, friends, mentors, and church community—thank you for covering me in prayer and love.

To every therapist, doctor, crisis responder, and compassionate stranger—thank you for seeing past the symptoms and treating the soul inside the struggle.

To The Mayflower and the holy ground of Room 235—thank you for holding both Mama's recovery and mine, a place where God spoke through symbols.

To every reader—thank you for holding my testimony in your hands. I pray it whispers hope to the wounded parts of you.

And finally, to the version of me who held on when life begged him to let go… I'm proud of you. You stayed. And because you stayed, this book lives.

ABOUT THE AUTHORS

Thoris Lamar Burt (pronounced "Toris") was born in Huntsville, Alabama—the 47-tag city that symbolically resurfaces throughout his testimony. A survivor, storyteller, and mental health advocate, Thoris began working for the federal government at the NCO Club on Redstone Arsenal at age fourteen, where he learned discipline, humility, and responsibility. His career spans decades in sales, leadership, technology, and insurance, yet his greatest work is found in the journey of healing, clarity, and purpose that shaped this book.

After surviving multiple mental health crises—including a near-fatal suicide attempt and a disorienting episode on May 8, 2025—Thoris embraced therapy, faith, and rest as sacred tools for restoration. His approval for SSDI at age forty-seven marked divine timing, aligning his life story with the symbolic number of his birthplace. Today, he is committed to helping others through transparency, vulnerability, and spiritual truth. This is his first book.

Carolyn Virginia Burt is a woman of grace, strength, and unwavering faith. A retired financial management analyst working for the federal government for thirty-five-plus years. She raised her children with discipline, love, and deep spiritual grounding. Her resilience during spinal surgery and recovery embodies the generational strength that runs through this story. Her relationship with Thoris—restored, renewed, and reconciled—stands as one of the central miracles of this testimony. This is her first book.

A CLOSING NOTE & RESOURCES

Why HE Kept Me is personal testimony, not professional advice. Nothing in it is meant to diagnose, treat, cure, or prevent any mental-health condition, and it is not medical, psychological, legal, or financial guidance. If you are struggling, please reach out to a qualified professional.

If you are in crisis, call or text the Suicide & Crisis Lifeline at 988, or call 911 and ask for a CIT-trained officer. If you are in immediate danger, contact local emergency services. Faith and professional care can walk together—please let them.

www.ingramcontent.com/pod-product-compliance
Lightning Source LLC
LaVergne TN
LVHW090353240926
848801LV00002B/26
* 9 7 9 8 9 9 6 4 9 7 9 1 1 *